3/21/11

Robert,

Thanks a million for
sharing your words of wisdom.
Since you love to read...
I would like to give you a copy of
my Million Dollar attitude Book.
would love to get your review after
you read it.
Keep inspiring.

with much Aloha,

Lori

Million Dollar Attitude

by

Joni B. Redick-Yundt

With Dr. Richard Schuttler

authorHOUSE®

AuthorHouse™
1663 Liberty Drive, Suite 200
Bloomington, IN 47403
www.authorhouse.com
Phone: 1-800-839-8640

First published by AuthorHouse 6/18/2007

ISBN: 978-1-4343-1827-5 (sc)

Library of Congress Control Number: 2007904073

Printed in the United States of America
Bloomington, Indiana

This book is printed on acid-free paper.

Contents

ACKNOWLEDGEMENTS

First of all, I want to thank God for everything that He has blessed me with, and for constantly being there for me and my family. He is the source of my strength, energy, health, and He has given me the courage to do what I needed to do.

To my husband, Tom Yundt: thank you for giving me the freedom to grow and expand my horizons. You have been a blessing in my life. Your unconditional love, support, trust, and understanding mean so much to me. I cherish every moment that we share. I love you.

To my son, Jason: thank you for being who you are, so caring, loving, and appreciative. Continue to learn all you can and to work towards your dreams. I am so proud of you. I remember when you first came into my life, how precious and small you were in my arms. Now, you're a grown man (six feet tall!) and ready to tackle the world.

To my daughter, Jessica: you are my beautiful, precious little angel---not so little anymore---you have been a bundle of joy to me. I treasure our happy moments together, especially when you helped me with my work. We laughed so much together; I enjoy your company. Now you are a grown young lady. Your love and understanding mean a lot to me.

To my parents, Lucia and Emilio Bumanglag, you have set an example for me that working hard leads to success. Thank you for being there for me when I needed your help and support. To my sisters, Lerry, Adela, and Nikky, you guys have been my cheerleaders! I thank you for your support, also.

To my sister Lu, even though you are no longer here, you're always with me. We have shared so many good times together---I miss you so much.

I am so grateful for three special people who provided their valuable time to help me prepare this manuscript. Their amazing team effort made this book a reality.

First, I thank Dr. Richard Schuttler for seeing something in my story and for believing that I have something to share with the world. I am truly honored that he saw the potential in me.

Second, I thank my husband again for partnering with me in this book and for being so instrumental in shaping its direction.

Third, I thank Sandy McKee. What can I say? She was a tremendous help in finishing my book. I appreciate her assistance, expertise, and friendship. It means so much to me. We spent long hours---day and night---without complaint. We had fun!

Special thanks go to Dr. Lawrence Tseu and Mr. Tai Khan, owner of Zaffron Indian Restaurant and Food Quality Analysts, who have consistently supported me for the last 20 years, from pageants to sponsorships for whatever I am involved in. I can't thank you enough for your generosity.

Another special thank you goes to Ken Simon, President and CEO of Menehune Water, and David Akina, Founder of Paradise Yellow Pages for your continued, never-ending support for nearly 10 years.

To Fletcher Jones of Mercedes Benz in Honolulu, thank you also for helping me for so many years. Your contribution to FAMES will always be remembered, as well as the support you have shown to the other organizations that I have been involved with.

To Bill Wyland, I really like when you call me "Buddy." You have been a tremendous help and I can always count on you. Thank you so much for your true friendship.

I am so grateful to the Fil-Am Courier newspaper, and to its Publisher, Mary Cordero, its columnist, Alice Busmente, its Editor,

Mila Medallon, for their support and belief in me. It has been my strength. Thank you for putting me on the cover!

Russell Tanoue, photographer, is owed a special thanks for making me extra beautiful for the book cover. Thank you for sharing your extraordinary talent.

To Jojo Serina, thank you so much for your dedication in designing the front and back covers for the book. Your talent and gifts are remarkable, and you are always so cheerful whenever I call, whether it is night or day.

I also appreciate the crew of the Atlantis Cruises Navatek I for allowing me to launch my book on your ship on the 4th of July, so that we can celebrate with a bang!

To all my friends and clients who believe in me and trust me to this day, you make me feel so good with all your compliments and encouragement. That keeps me going!

Thank you to everyone who has taken part in making my dreams come true. God bless you all.

Joni

INTRODUCTION

**Joni believes: "Day or night, rain or shine, far or near,
I will be there. Work or play, I'm ready any day."**

I decided to write this book simply because I love to help people. Friends often ask me for advice, for help, or for a sympathetic ear when they need to talk. Sometimes they are not happy or content with their lives. I encourage them as much as I can.

It is truly a great feeling when they tell me, "Joni, you're an inspiration! You make me feel good just talking to you."

You see, I believe in them, much like Mary Kay Ash and my Sales Director, Perlita Ancheta, believed in me. Their examples gave me courage. They saw something in me that I didn't see. I want to do the same for the people in my life.

I reflect back on all the experiences I have had---good and bad---and I believe I have something to share that might make a difference in the lives of others.

I can tell them not to worry about humble beginnings---mine were as humble as they come!

I tell them not to worry about obstacles and disappointments along the way---I've faced my share of those!

I can tell them not to be derailed by negativity and doubts---I've fought against those all my life!

I can tell them not to be discouraged by failure---I've failed big, but it has led me to win big.

I can tell them to have courage, to be creative, to do something positive. I can tell them to volunteer in the community. It feels so good! It's energizing when you help others.

But, most importantly, I can tell them they have choices: they can decide to be happy; they can decide to be successful. It starts with attitude.

For those who are looking for the same advice that I give to my friends, please read on. I pray that something in my story will inspire you to greater heights, and that you will live each day with a *MILLION DOLLAR ATTITUDE!*

Joni B. Redick-Yundt

JONI'S MILLION DOLLAR ATTITUDE

In order to have a *Million Dollar Attitude*, follow these keys to success:

M – Make things happen
I – Imagine and visualize your dreams
L – Love one another
L – Live a life of serenity
I – Initiate action
O – Open your mind
N – Never quit – embrace adversity

D – Dare to live
O – Organize
L – Live life to the fullest
L – Learn and grow
A – Act on your dreams, do not procrastinate
R – Resourceful and get results

A – Absorb knowledge and wisdom
T – Take it to the top
T – Teamwork
I – Inspire others
T – Together we can do it
U – Undaunted; perfectionisim is paralysis
D – Don't be sensitive or defensive
E – Energetic, excited, enthusiastic; exercise and have fun

by Joni B. Redick-Yundt

CHAPTER 1
Early Training And Preparation

Joni believes: "Get up, get out, and go!"

**"Even a child is known by his actions,
by whether his conduct is pure and right."
Proverbs 20:11 (NIV)**

Early in the Philippines

The "4th of July" is not celebrated in the Philippines with a holiday and exploding fireworks as is customary in the United States, so when I was born on July 4th in the province of Cagayan, Luzon, in the Philippines, it was a quiet day. Now that I live in the United States, I am blessed and fortunate to celebrate both Independence Day and my birthday each year with fireworks.

My parents, Emilio and Lucia Bumanglag, raised five daughters: Leriza, Lu, me, Adela, and Nikky. My earliest memories were of helping my father give a bath to the family's carabao in the river near our house. A carabao is a water buffalo and is one of the national symbols of the Philippines. It is a large, gentle creature used for plowing the fields and doing other farm chores. At the time, I did not know it, but by joining in the work at this early age,

I was preparing myself to lead a productive life. In fact, I did not even think of it as work; I was having fun!

When I was two years old, I snuck away from my mother who was outside the house. I went into the kitchen, sat on the floor, and cut off half of my hair. My mother walked in, witnessed all the hair on the floor and became upset. My hair was short on one side! I did not understand. Looking back, even at a young age I wanted to look my best, but as seen through my own eyes - not the eyes of others. The early days of my life were foundational in creating who I am today.

At the age of two, I moved to the province of Balacad to live with one of my aunts. My older sister, Lu, moved in with another aunt in Laoag City, and the rest of the family moved to another town nearby. The family did this because my parents were not able to financially support all of us. My aunt did not have any children and her husband was in the United States. My aunt was able to help my parents provide for me. I stayed with her in Balacad until I was eleven years old. In the Philippines, it was not uncommon for a child to live with an aunt and uncle, as the extended family is part of the Filipino culture – one big happy family who loves and helps one another.

I have many wonderful memories from my youth. Although we were not rich with money, we were rich in spirit and I was a happy child. My aunt and I lived in a simple one-bedroom house in the country. We did not have the now common luxuries such as running water, electricity, or television. We did have a battery-powered radio and I enjoyed listening to it. I remember wondering how in the world they managed to fit those little people into that radio!

The "comfort room" as we called the toilet, was found outside the main house. Our house did not have any running water. Toilet paper was also nonexistent, so we made our own with a creative technique. We would take old newspaper, and then---this part is important---crumple the paper repeatedly to soften it up; this was our toilet paper! Unfortunately, the softening up process was more ceremonial than effective and the paper was not so soft. Ouch!

The Journey to School

In retrospect, living a simple life in the provinces was good for me. I learned about discipline and routine. A typical weekday would include getting up by 6:00 a.m., meeting with cousins and neighbors, and then walking the seven miles to elementary school. This was not an easy early morning stroll. We had several hills to climb along the dirt path while carrying heavy books and school supplies. We would make this trek every school day, whether it was sunny, drizzling a little, or raining like a full-blown monsoon! We would grab a banana leaf and use that to protect ourselves like an umbrella. This kept us dry. After school, the cycle would repeat itself and we would once again, rain or shine, grab our heavy books and begin the seven-mile hike back home. As young children, we were in good physical shape!

The journey to and from school was a great aerobic exercise and an adventure also. In the provinces, there was a history of insurgent activity and kidnappings. As we were walking to and from the school, if we heard a vehicle or motorcycle, we would run down the hill off the path and hide behind the bushes and trees so the *bad guys* could not get us. Adding to the danger were the snakes that would cross our dirt path and scurry away into the brush. The Philippines is home to many venomous snakes like the King Cobra, pit vipers, and bamboo snakes. Naturally, we would scream if we saw one, then we would continue on our way.

I enjoyed school. We would wait patiently for our teachers to arrive and would then volunteer to take their books to the classroom. Once inside, the entire class would line up and greet the teachers with "Hi, Sir!" or "Hi, Ma'am!" This was our normal way of showing respect to our teachers and elders. Then, the student assigned to *Bell Duty* would ring the huge bell, a relic of World War II, in the courtyard. The entire student body, Grades One to Six, would run into the grassy courtyard area in front of the flagpole and we would together sing our National Anthem. Often I was fortunate to be asked to lead the anthem, in the manner of a choir director.

Our typical school day was long. Classes started at 8:00 a.m. and continued until 5:00 p.m. I enjoyed the learning, but I had a difficult time with physical education. We were often made to run or jog and I was usually the last one to finish. I developed a dislike for running. I will never do a marathon!

Each school day we had break times for recess and lunch. I remember that my cousin would bring chocolate candies from their small family store and ask me to help sell them to my schoolmates and teachers while she was playing. This did not seem fair, she playing and I working, but since she was older and bigger, I went along with the plan. I managed to get paid in chocolate, so it was okay. Those were my first sales and my first commissions!

Truthfully, I was not overjoyed about reading and studying, but I liked the way we tended the school garden. It was fun to go through the process of planting the seeds, watering them every morning before class, and watching as the seedlings developed into edible food! As part of our home economics class, we would cook these fruits and veggies for lunch, sometimes sharing with the teachers. It was rewarding to see our successful results and to share it with others.

Every year, from first grade to sixth, I was awarded a ribbon for being the *Most Tidy*. At that time, I was not even sure what "tidy" meant, but I enjoyed receiving the honor and the ribbon. I guess this was a preview of what was yet to come!

Twice a year, at Christmas and graduation, our school sponsored a program featuring dancing, singing, dramatic skits, and speeches. Our families and friends would attend, and sometimes the Mayor or Governor would also attend. I enjoyed dancing the traditional Filipino dances and was often asked to train and coach the other students in learning these dance steps properly. When it came time to perform, I was considered the "star dancer" and had the honor of being in the front row of the entourage. I had some experience at home with dancing. Whenever there was a birthday party or family event, I would be invited to dance. As I danced, people would toss coins. Later, I gathered the coins and put them into my piggy bank. That was as sophisticated as my financial planning was in those days!

Once arriving home from school, I washed-up before dinner by scooping water from a large tub of well water. I would have dinner, do homework by the light of a kerosene lamp, and then went to sleep *the sleep of the righteous*. A comfy bed with a mattress would have been nice, but I had to make do with a concrete floor, a mat, a blanket, and a pillow! While this seems primitive, like camping full-time, as kids we did not mind it, then again – I did not know any different either!

Toys and Games

Having virtually no money and few store-bought toys did not stop us from making our own fun. Whenever the full moon was out, the neighborhood gang, most of them cousins, would congregate and have a marathon session of hide-and-seek. My aunt had a small shack next to the house which was used to store the rice stalks we would harvest. The shack became our "clubhouse." One of our favorite games was to make pretend money by taking old newspapers and folding and cutting the paper into money-sized pieces, which we would then use in "business transactions." We would not necessarily trade anything, we would just pretend with the pretend money, and that was fine with us. If we did "buy and sell," we would improvise with such common items as rubber bands, stones, and marbles. That was all we had, but we were happy.

Jeepney to the Market

Weekends were a major adventure. I would jump out of bed early, while it was still dark, eagerly expecting the day ahead. My aunt and I grabbed a quick breakfast and then, without delay, we ventured out into the fields to harvest tomatoes, string beans, eggplant, and sweet potatoes. We bundled and bagged them, and walked down to the jeepney stop.

A jeepney is a popular form of public transportation in the Philippines. They were originally made from surplus jeeps that the U.S. military left after World War II. The jeepney was "value" transportation with metal roofs, open windows, and no air conditioning or comforts. The few seats they had were usually taken, so it was "standing room only" inside and a half dozen or more folks hanging on the outside. To add even more local color to the experience, more often than not there was a gaggle of chickens on the roof raising quite a commotion for most of the forty-five minute ride to the market. Sometimes there was a conductor on the jeepney who would collect the fare, a fraction of one peso, very affordable, and who would also relay to the driver when a passenger needed to exit. The passenger would initiate his request by loudly banging on the side of the jeepney. The loud banging was a requirement since with all the commotion of the jeepney's engine, people talking, and the chicken noise from above, it would take a serious effort to get the attention of the conductor. It was an art form getting around the provinces in the jeepney.

The jeepney would stop along the bumpy, dusty, dirt road whenever there were folks on the side of the road looking for a lift. Eventually, there came a point when no more people could be crammed into the jeepney, and then we would continue nonstop to the market. Even without periodic stops along the way, the jeepney would labor to attain a maximum speed of roughly 30 miles per hour. Any faster would be suicide due to the condition of the dirt road and the frequency and depth of the monster potholes.

Once we arrived at the open market, we would lay down a blanket on the ground and place our veggies out for sale. Like many others, we were part-time vendors. The part-timers sold clay pots, fish, and fresh vegetables. The covered area of the market was reserved for the daily vendors, so we sat in the hot sun all day. Customers would walk by, and if interested, start to bargain for our wares. At the tender age of six, I watched my aunt negotiate with the customers. She was very good at this. We stayed until we sold everything, and then grabbed a quick lunch in the covered market area before heading off to the jeepney station. One of my favorite parts of the day was when my auntie would reward me with an ice cream cone from the push cart vendors at the jeepney station. This would get me energized for the jeepney ride back home.

Paddle-Beating the Laundry

Another favorite weekend chore was doing the laundry. We placed the dirty laundry in a wicker basket and balanced this on top of our heads (just like you see on documentaries today). Who needed yoga? We had balance! To get to the neighborhood "Laundromat" required a thirty-minute walk into the jungle to a spot where there was a waterfall and small pool. We used bar soap and rubbed the clothes together by hand to get them clean. For stubborn stains, we took a paddle and simply beat the darn stains out of the clothes. Hey, we didn't have Spray 'n Wash! Besides, it worked.

We placed the clean clothes on large rocks that faced the sun. While we waited for them to dry, we gathered wild mushrooms. We were not aware that there were "good" mushrooms and "not so good" mushrooms. We ate pretty much everything. Also, there were many fruit trees around the waterfall, and we gathered guava, mangoes, and other tropical fruits. We came prepared with a tin cup to gather eggs of the large ants that seemed to like hanging out in the trees, taking care not to get stung by the critters. My aunt would later fry them up. They made an excellent protein side dish. Yummy!

Harvesting Rice

My father's parents owned land in the area where we lived. Some of it was planted with rice. When the rice was ready to reap, it was "all hands on deck" to assist with the harvest. Cousins, aunts, and uncles of all ages worked together in the fields. We used really sharp machetes to cut the rice stalks and then we bundled the rice stalks together. Once we had cleared an area of the rice stalks, there would be numerous grasshoppers hopping about wondering what happened to their shelter. We, likewise, would hop around and catch the little buggers, immediately roasting them on a small fire made especially for that purpose. Believe it or not, everyone really enjoyed this, including yours truly. The grasshoppers tasted like shrimp. Crunchy!

Missing My Family

Although my life with my aunt was full and fun, there were times that I grew terribly lonesome for my family. I did not have anyone to read me bedtime stories, or sisters to play and fight with. However, every couple of months, my father would come on his bicycle and pick me up. I rode on the handlebars as he pedaled down the dirt road to the house where he, my mother, and most of my sisters stayed. Lu would come in from the city as well and we had the family together for a weekend.

We sisters played endlessly and it was great being with all of them. I recall how we used to walk on Dad's back to massage him. When he got up, we would hang from his arms, legs and neck and giggle uncontrollably. We had fun together. When mom went to the river to do the laundry, we would accompany her and gather clams and seaweed for dinner. Being in the provinces, there were a lot of superstitions, the main one being that vampires roamed the night. Apparently, Mom was really concerned. Before bedtime she gave all of us a few cloves of garlic to keep them at bay.

I remember how my sister Lu and I, only eight months apart in age, had a special bond much like twins. She and I were distributed to outlying relatives, so we both shared much the same feelings of separation from the rest of the family. I recall the two of us sitting in back of Dad's house near the cucumber patch, where the chickens were running around. We talked about how much we missed each other.

On those special weekends, Dad would sometimes treat all five sisters to a special night out. He would take us to the *cinehan*, or movie house. Since he was paying for the tickets, he would, unfortunately, get to choose the movie. I say unfortunately because the movies he would select, that all us six girls (5 daughters and Mom) would then have to watch, were either World War II movies or, even worse, Bruce Lee-style kung fu movies. I think Dad was hoping to have a son! So, we five daughters and Mom humored him on his choice of movies.

Often, when I got ready for Dad to take me back to my aunt's house, Mom would give me a new dress that she sewed. It was a kind of going-away present, until the next time. I clutched it happily all the way as we pedaled back.

Philippines to the United States

In 1969, Dad traveled to Hawaii because his sister, who was already living in Hawaii, had petitioned for his immigration. Dad decided to take the chance and come to Hawaii with the hopes of securing employment, sending money back to us, and then bringing the family to join him. He found a good-paying job in the construction trades and sent back money for us while at the same time saving to bring us to the United States.

A few years later, he came back to Philippines and following a joyous reunion, proceeded to build a new house for the family, next to my aunt's house. This new house was something else, with an indoor flushing toilet, a hand pump to bring water up from the well, and a large elevated water tank to enable us to take showers! Hallelujah!

Once the new house was ready, the entire family moved in, with both sister Lu and I gladly returning to the home. Having the five sisters under one roof was a lot of fun, although Mom may not agree with this assessment. We were not only under one roof, but were also all bunched in one family room during many hours of the day. This certainly made for interesting moments.

When her "out-of-control" daughters, as my mother put it, needed to be quieted down, Mom would employ her famous, incredibly strong, pincer movement. She would pinch the offending sister on the belly, and thus evoke a rather loud "Ouch!" from the one needing the discipline.

Even though Dad had hired someone to help Mom with all of the various chores, Mom really carried the ball for us during these years, and we all believe that Mom is a saint to have put up with all of us rabble-rousing daughters!

As we settled in the new house, we felt like royalty, even though we still had some of the not-so-royal chores that came with living in the provinces. Tending to the chickens was a chore that was actually fun: feeding them with corn and rice, watching the baby chicks hatch, and playing with the baby chicks in my palm. That was neat. One of the less royal of the chores was tending to the three pigs that we raised out back. Fortunately, one of my sisters would usually pick up the piggy poop. I did, too, from time to time, but I never really learned to enjoy that particular chore. Not that I am anti-piggy.

I recall when living with my auntie earlier, we had a pregnant piggy that gave birth to eight baby piglets. The mommy pig elected to raise and nurse the little piglets underneath the house. I loved playing with the little piglets, and I think that these were my "Barbie dolls." I think I had more fun with these little critters that I possibly could have had with a Malibu Barbie---no comparison. In stark contrast to our contemporary Blackberry and iPod culture, we did not have nifty electronic devices. For that matter, we did not have electricity!

Fortunately for us, we did not know you needed such things to be happy, and happy we were. Instead of digital sound, for example, we had a rich symphony of sounds courtesy of the baby piglets oinking constantly from underneath the house. This combined with the cackling chickens from the yard, and was accompanied by the Ilocano and Tagalog *Top Forty* songs emanating from the decidedly Lo-Fi battery-powered transistor radio. Beat that for audio entertainment!

As the family moved up in the world, Dad purchased a jeepney, appropriately named "Five Sisters." This particularly colorful jeepney was a source of pride for the family. This vehicle was large, and was a steady source of income for us, as the jeepney route was between our province and downtown Laoag City. Our cousin was the "designated driver" and he would regularly come to the house in the evening with bags and bags of coins. We sisters gathered round the table and took great pleasure in counting the proceeds. Mom and Dad would take the money, and while encouraging all of us to study hard in school, would tell us they were depositing the money in the bank for our college fund.

While Dad was in the Philippines, he formally petitioned, through the immigration office, for all of us to immigrate over to Hawaii. Mom and Dad took me aside and asked if I would prefer to come with all of them to Hawaii, or if I would rather have my auntie adopt me and stay in the Philippines. I was very fond of my aunt, and recall how she would cuddle with me before I drifted off to sleep every night, and the decision to say good-bye to her, and stay with the family was not an easy one. She really took care of me in my early years.

So, with the plan in place for all of us to immigrate to Hawaii, we would take periodic visits to the big city of Manila, and visit the Immigration offices, an exercise that was normally an all day event. Waiting in lines, then waiting in more lines, then waiting in, yes, even more lines, was the deal at Immigration. It seemed that the bureaucratic process moved with the speed of a glacier. After many of these sojourns to Manila, during which we would stay at another auntie's house, we, finally, after three years, received the "Okay" from the Immigration Services, both Philippine and American. Hurrah!

Aloha Hawaii!

We packed up our possessions that consisted of a few articles of clothing and not much else, and headed for the airport in Manila to embark on a new journey. This was our first ride on an airplane. We did not know quite how to react to such an overwhelming adventure. We did not have much money and Mom was concerned about how she would feed all of us while traveling on the plane. She, and all of us, was greatly relieved to learn that the meals would be served to us free of charge. Hey, this travel thing was kind of fun!

Once we arrived in our new home, Honolulu, Hawaii, Dad took us to a house in Aiea that he had purchased with his sister. The house was a simple up-and-down dwelling, nothing fancy. But, the fact that all of us were together in Honolulu was amazing! The five sisters once again shared one bedroom, and once again mom had to utilize her famous "pincer on the belly" to sort-of keep us in line.

Dad, also, had seen no need to change his ways, and so on weekend nights he would take us all to the *cinehan*, which in our new surroundings was a drive-in theater. This was a real adventure for us; such a huge screen! And popcorn! This was just way too cool at that time. One thing that did not change, unfortunately, was the choice of movies. We watched World War II movies or Bruce Lee Kung-fu movies. I will hesitantly admit that I learned to enjoy the Bruce Lee movies in time. Ayeee-yah! I do recall one instance; however, when we were able to talk Dad into taking us all to a non-kung-fu, non-World-War-II movie. We saw "Superman" on the big screen. I loved America!

High School in Hawaii

Upon arriving in America, at the age of fourteen, I was enrolled in 10th grade at Aiea High School. This level seemed appropriate, since under the Philippine system there were six grades of elementary followed by four year high school, with no Middle

School. So, entering 10th grade seemed logical. After my first year, the school administration assessed my abilities and said that I could skip the 11th grade and go directly to 12th grade. I was somewhat ambivalent about this, feeling proud but concerned because of my young age and my "petiteness," not to mention leaving my sister Lu one grade behind me. Nonetheless, I elected to go directly into the senior year of high school at the age of fifteen!

This worked out fine, as I managed to finish Driver's Education training (first one in the family, I might add). I am sure that the driver's training teaching staff has not yet forgotten the group of us that took that class together, as we would routinely bring green mango and bagaoong, (salted fermented shrimp paste), which tastes great, but smells, well, not so great. Our driving teacher would give us really dirty looks, open the windows, and mention that the smell reminded him of a dead rat. Yum!

Perhaps more importantly, I secured a spot on the Principal's List, and the Honor Roll, so I think my senior year worked out fine. Receiving these honors "erased" in my mind some of the classmates that thought it funny to make jokes about my family name. I noticed that these types were conspicuously absent from the Honor Rolls and Principal's Lists. Ah, sweet revenge.

Especially sweet, since we had a special immigrant's class made up of mostly Filipino students, but with other ethnic groups. We were aware of our status within the school's social pecking order, being essentially strangers in a strange land. By and large, we were more motivated to excel, I believe.

We also developed a bond between one another, and learned to laugh at our sometimes awkward predicaments together. Some of my closest friends in life came from this environment, including Elena Lopez. We are still friends to this day.

The teachers of the immigrant classes spent some time in trying to improve our pronunciation of the English language, and they were met with "checkered" success. One notable failure, which brought constant laughter to all, was our collective inability to get the seemingly simple phrase "bus stop" correct. We, for whatever reason, could not get that right. Instead, we would pronounce it as "bus is stopped." Following this mispronunciation, there would be uproar of laughter from all. We learned to develop a good sense of humor about such things, although I think we drove our teacher insane. This teacher, a big, good-hearted *haole* man (Caucasian fella), was amazingly patient with us and usually laughed along with us, so we really liked having him as our teacher.

CHAPTER 2
Working As A Young Woman

Joni believes: "Create your own destiny."

"She sets about her work vigorously;
her arms are strong for her tasks."
Proverbs 31:17 (NIV)

Del Monte

I had done my share of chores within the family, both in the Philippines and in Honolulu, and was actually looking forward to the time when I could enter the workforce and earn money. When my sister Lu, a scant eight months older than I, turned sixteen, she and I marched down to the Del Monte pineapple processing plant and applied for a summer job. They accepted Lu's application, but in my case, I was told that I could submit an application, but could not begin work until I turned sixteen. I was disappointed that I could not join Lu in our first paying job. But, I accepted the rules and vowed to return right after my sixteenth birthday. I would have gone to their employment office on my birthday, but they, like most other places of business, were closed on July 4th, which is my birthday.

On July 5th, I appeared at the office, was given the go-ahead, and started work on that day. I just could not wait to start work! I think the main reason was that I wanted to share this experience with my sister Lu. For this new adventure, this brand new foray into the working world, Lu and I would rise and shine at 3:00 a.m., and our Dad, who worked construction, would drop us off at Del Monte at 4:00 a.m. Needless to say, it was still very dark at that hour.

"Packing pineapple" was the job description, and it was accurate. Ten of us packers would be situated around a conveyor belt with already cored and sliced pineapple making a steady procession past our workstations. Our job was to select "only the best" pineapple slices and then place them into the can. This was not considered skilled labor by any means, but Lu and I had loads of fun doing this.

Whenever the conveyor would slow down, or we had to wait for more pineapple, inevitably the entire group would start singing that favorite campfire song "Ninety-Nine Bottles of Beer on the Wall." I am not sure how that tradition got started, but, that was part of the job.

One of the highlights of that experience was my first payday. Since that was before direct deposit became the rage, we all had to stand in line and wait our turn to get our checks. I was too excited for words, waiting for a rather long time in line, while thinking of what to do with my first check. Hmmm.. Put some money in the bank, and more importantly, get some new clothes! My weakness, both then and now.

My Mustang

Of the five of us, I was the lone sister who had a burning desire to drive a car. Dad tried to teach my sister Lu how to drive, but she became scared. So, when I came of age, raring to go, my parents thought it a good idea to get me a car to help with the going to and from college and work. To my surprise, one day Mom and Dad asked me to come outside for a minute. Parked outside the house was a beautiful, green, 1966 Mustang. It was mine. Wow! This car was so cool that I hopped into it and became a real driver without delay---and also without a driver's license. Details, details. Off I went - with my newfound freedom, but eventually I thought it prudent to actually get a driver's license.

My first driving test went very well, as I had been driving the car for some time, except for a minor detail regarding a maneuver that the man called "parallel parking." I was not so practiced at this, and so in spite of my otherwise stellar performance, I was busted. I did not pass. Arghh! So, with some instruction from my dad in the parking lot of the community college (punctuated with "Ouch! You would have hit the other car!), and hours upon hours of practice, I found the courage to once again take the driver's exam. This time, success!!

College Days

At the age of sixteen, I began my college career at Leeward Community College in Pearl City, Hawaii majoring in accounting. I am not exactly sure why I chose that particular field, except that I was good in Math. I had no early college guidance or set direction. I wish I had. I believe if I did, I would have been able to achieve so much more.

I attended college during the day and then went to Pearlridge Hospital where I worked as a dietician's aide in the evenings. Many times during my rounds at the hospital, I passed by the Emergency Room and got a glimpse of some gruesome scenes involving much blood. It made me feel sick and I was glad that I was not working in the E.R. It takes a special person to cope with life-and-death situations on a daily basis. That was not for me.

It is interesting how events happen, though, in one's life – especially in retrospect. I became bored with accounting classes, but found I enjoyed working in different areas of the hospital. Thinking there would likely be a place for me to work that did

NOT involve the E.R., I decided to go into nursing. This was more logical as I liked helping others, especially the elderly. Imagine my shock and surprise when my nursing internship called for me to work in the Emergency Room! They liked the speed at which I worked and how well I associated with everyone. The supervisor of the E.R. heard this and offered me the position. By this time, I had somewhat overcome my earlier hesitation to be around blood and I accepted the job.

My first night at the E.R. as a real nurse, just out of school, was unforgettable. My first patient was a man who had been in a tragic car accident. He came to us bloody and in bad shape. Sadly, he passed away shortly after arriving at the hospital. I was asked to clean the body after the doctors had tried to save him.

Next, a large and heavy Samoan woman came in who had suffered a major heart attack. Unfortunately, she also passed away within minutes of arriving in the E.R. It was a sobering and discouraging start. But, I had to shake it off because the next patient was a teenager who had been in a serious car accident. He was bloody and screaming when he arrived, and throughout the initial examination. I had to transfer him around the hospital to the X-Ray department and the operating room. I tried to offer comfort as best I could, but it was not easy because of the pain the young man was experiencing. Fortunately, the doctors were able to save him and it was a relief to end the first night on a positive note.

Victory over the Cash Register

Many people in Hawaii have to take multiple jobs to support themselves and their families; and I was no exception. While I studied nursing at Kapiolani Community College, I worked at Leed's Shoe Store in downtown Honolulu, near Chinatown. For those not familiar with Honolulu's Chinatown, this is a culturally fascinating area that is hustle and bustle during the daytime with shoppers and office workers. At night it attracts a crowd of more dubious character, especially near the infamous Hotel Street where the "mahus" (transvestites) frequent.

I was naïve about the whole "mahu" situation. Many times an attractive woman (or so I thought) would come into the store and end up buying four or five pairs of shoes. I was bewildered at first by the baritone voice and the Size 10 shoes. I told myself, "What the heck?" I figured out that these customers were special and it wasn't my place to judge. Besides, they were nice people and I enjoyed "talking story" with them. For whatever reason, I was effective in selling them many shoes!

I discovered quickly that I was good at sales, but bad at working the "ten key" cash register. My manager had mixed feelings about my job performance. She would grab the shoe boxes out of my hands, slam them on the counter, and ring them up herself. She pounded the register keys so hard! I was embarrassed because of the way she acted in front of the customers, but I watched quietly and respectfully.

I told myself I had to learn how to operate the cash register quickly. At times I worried that my exceptional sales ability might not compensate for my less-than-stellar operation of the cash register. However, my manager eventually found the patience to give me additional training and support. With time and practice, like most things in my life, I became good at working the cash register.

I noticed the manager's behavior changed drastically for the better once I knew how to use the cash register. I remember how good it felt to have won her over. I was grateful that she changed from being ready to fire me to appreciating my determination to learn. It felt empowering to go from being a borderline employee to being viewed as a valuable employee. The result was definitely worth my efforts.

My Plate is Never Full

It might seem to most people that my plate was full, with working and going to school. But, I have always thrived on having challenges in my life. I do not think in terms of limitations. Plus, if I did things quickly and efficiently, I found I could do more.

Another example of this is that while I was attending nursing school and working at the shoe store, I also was studying to become an airline reservation specialist. My sister Lu and I always yearned to become flight attendants, as that job seemed glamorous to us. The problem was that both Lu and I were too petite for the airlines and could not meet the minimum height requirements without standing on our toes and jumping a bit. Besides, our mother did not approve of that career path because of her concerns about the airplane crashing. But, this did not deter us too much, as we figured we could be involved in the travel industry by becoming reservation specialists. We could get the glamorous airline perk of flying free, if nothing else. And, as if this was not enough, in my spare time I was taking guitar lessons! I think it is safe to say I was "multitasking" way before it became trendy.

Arizona

I was married when I just had turned 20 years old. Unfortunately, the marriage did not last. Life must go on. We moved to Arizona to see how I might like mainland living. I kept an open mind, and upon arriving in Arizona, proceeded to look for employment. I thought the people there were nice, but quite a bit different from the islands. For their part, they seemed confused about my ancestry and race. Chinese? Mexican? American Indian? Take your pick!

I remember one time we were taking a break together, having some ice cream, and I mentioned my favorite brands of ice cream made in the Philippines. This prompted the question, "Oh you have ice cream over there?" Oh, dear.

One thing that I really missed was the near complete absence of rice at any and all restaurants. Living in the Philippines and Hawaii, I had gotten used to having rice at breakfast, lunch, and dinner. I was at a loss for words when a waitress would ask, "How would you like your potatoes: baked or French fried?"

I would answer along the lines of, "Do you have rice?" This would prompt an "are-you-from-this-planet?" look. I preferred rice, so I would take cooked rice wrapped in foil and stash it in my purse whenever I went out to eat.

At the top of my list in the new surroundings was a search for employment. With my education, nursing experience, E.R. and clinic experience, I figured that getting a good-paying job would be fairly easy. A chiropractic clinic hired me soon after my arrival in Arizona, and things went really well---at least for the first three days.

While I was more than acceptable in most of the job tasks, and received compliments from patients, there was one troubling aspect of my job performance that caused me to be, um, terminated. In other words: "shown the door," "canned," "sacked," or perhaps "fired." Oops.

I attribute this somewhat unfortunate outcome to karma. Allow me to explain. The "area needing improvement" was my woeful skills in typing and transcribing. Unfortunately, I had told them at the interview that I could type. And, I could. But, I did not mention that I typed "really slow."

I figured that they would not mind so much. After all, I had taken typing class in college, and had passed with some help from my sister Lu. This is where the "karma" thing comes into play. You see, Lu and I were often mistaken for twin sisters. She was my height, shape, and our features were so similar that we were tempted at times to do things such as, well, um, substitute for each other on occasions. When in college, one semester was rather heavy for me, and so I had asked Lu to take my typing final exam because she was a lot better than I at typing. I was afraid that if I took the final, I would fail and have to take the darn class over again. So, Lu took the exam for me, aced it, and I got a good grade! What a deal!

Now, years later, my typing karma came back to haunt me. Oh, no! The chiropractors became very impatient with my slow-boat-to-china typing skills, and so they fired me. Contrite, but undeterred, I began the search for job Number Two.

I went to an employment agency, and with my qualifications and experience, they found an opening in a medical clinic and spoke to them on my behalf. The agent and I felt that I would be a good fit, and so we were hoping to get an offer from the clinic. Unfortunately, the clinic called the agent with "we have hired someone else." The agent called me to inform me of the bad news.

At that point, I gave the clinic a call to ask them why I did not get the job. The following day, I heard from the irritated agent, "You are not supposed to call them directly! That is our job." I responded that I was just curious, since I seemed a perfect fit. They said, "Don't worry; we will find you another one."

And, they did. A group of six dermatologists hired me, and things went very well from the start. Even though there was a three month probationary period, I learned quickly from the start, and earned a raise after only one month. My efforts were appreciated at the clinic, and I enjoyed working there tremendously.

One day, after I had been at the derma group for six months or so, one of the doctor's friends dropped by to say hello. Coincidentally, this doctor was part of the clinic that did not want to hire me. My dermatologist employer raved and raved about me and introduced me to his friend. I recognized the clinic name. I responded with, "Oh, so you are the ones that did not want me. Well, I told you so." Karma works both ways.

There were some bright spots in the mainland U.S. adventure, but at the end of the day, Hawaii called. I missed my family, the islands, the food (rice!), the climate, and the culture. This is a common experience with islanders; they miss their unique culture when traveling and seem to migrate back if at all possible.

My Health Guru

Back in Honolulu, I took a night job at Pearlridge Hospital's Emergency Room, and in addition, took a day job at Dr. Roger Ogata's clinic full time. This might seem excessive, two full-time positions, but this is not an issue for me; I am a born multitasker.

Dr. Roger Ogata soon became my favorite health guru, as he had a remarkable energy level, never seemed to get stressed, or get angry. His attitude was "Why get upset? I don't need ulcers or high blood pressure." Dr. Ogata seemed to never get sick, and when I inquired as to how he did this, he would give me advice in terms of preventative medicine, multivitamins, and positive attitude.

We had a separate lab, with lots of high tech machines, and Dr. Ogata taught me how to operate this intimidating equipment since our lab technician got sick quite often. In addition, Dr. Ogata gave me some tips in drawing blood. I was not too bad at this, but even though I had training and some experience, I was probably considered average in this skill. A challenging patient, one with deep veins, would sometimes have a black and blue mark as an aftermath of my hunting expedition (where is that darn vein?). However, when Dr. Ogata was done teaching me, I had elevated this skill to an art form. Just do not ask me to type anything!

In Retrospect

Looking back, I think this was the beginning of my *Million Dollar Attitude*. At least, it was the beginning of my realization that attitude can change everything and that I can accomplish what I set out to do. The power of identifying my passion and applying it with focus, as well as my desire to help others achieve their full potential in life was not realized until much later in my life. But, this was the point where I became mindful that I had a degree of control over my destiny.

I CAN

I look in the mirror and ask myself
What do I want to be?
What do I want to have and do?
The choice is up to me.
Created in the image of God
The Bible says we are.
And with God all things are possible;
So reach for the highest star.
First, we have to set our goals,
Then create and work our plan.
And when doubts and fears get in the way
Keep on saying 'I can.'
Face each day with confidence;
Stand tall, with your head held high.
Believe in yourself and you'll make it.
You can, if only you'll try.
Dare to hold fast to your dream
While you do what you must do.
Always keep your eye on your vision;
The wisdom inside will guide you.
Take action, get out of the shadows
And step out into the sun!
For the only race you can win in life
Is the race that you have run.
We measure success by money and wealth,
But so much better by far
Is the success of feeling the strength inside
When you know who you really are.
Each one of us is a special person;
We're all one of a kind,
With untapped potential that awakens
When you learn how to use your mind.
Now when I look in the mirror
I finally love what I see.
I can do anything I really want to -
Thank God I'm Me!!!

Author Unknown

CHAPTER 3
Mary Kay - Making The Impossible Possible

Joni believes: "Turn your passion into
action, and make it happen."

"...if you have faith as small as a mustard seed,
you can say to this mountain,
'Move from here to there' and it will move.
Nothing will be impossible for you."
Matthew 17:20 (NIV)

Mary Kay

I was not blessed with the skin of a supermodel. At sixteen
years old, I was a typical teenage girl whose complexion was not
perfect. Yet, I wanted it to be. One of the nurses at the hospital was
a friend of my mother. She was also a Mary Kay beauty consultant.
She recommended I try Mary Kay's skin care products as she saw
just how bad my complexion was. My mother knew that it was
important to me to look good. She encouraged me to take her
friend's suggestion. I was desperate, so I did! She gave me my first
facial right there at the Nurses' station.

The beauty consultant showed me proper techniques to take
care of my skin. More importantly, I learned the right products to

use. My mother bought the entire Mary Kay skin care program and several other glamour products for me. In 1979, spending $175 for a teenager's complexion was not common, especially with money so tight. I was lucky!

Neither my mother nor I knew anything about dermatology. I am thankful that my mother had the insight to do something about my severe teenage acne. I started using the Mary Kay products morning and night, just as the instructions stipulated. I followed the instructions perfectly, but for the first two months that I used these products, my acne became worse! I was heartbroken. I called my Mary Kay beauty consultant and complained that my skin was getting worse, and screamed that I was going to stop using the products and I wanted a refund!

She replied, "Oh, no! That means it is working!" I responded, "What do you mean it is working?"

She explained the products are cleaning deep under my skin and this temporary backslide is to be expected. She encouraged me to continue. Since she was a nurse and I was only a sixteen-year old girl, I figured that she would know better than I. But, I was scared that I had done something that would leave me with acne scars for life!

I prayed, kept faith in the product, and followed the directions exactly as provided. I was determined that these products would make a difference – they had to! After several more weeks, I noticed that my acne was not as bad and my confidence was growing. Then, steady improvement followed. I guess the beauty consultant knew what she was talking about! While I still had some acne, it was mild and many people commented about the difference in my skin. I was gaining more confidence as I saw changes occurring.

A major turning point early in my life

After a couple of years of using the skin care products, the nurse who introduced me to Mary Kay products was no longer available. When I was working at St. Francis Hospital, I found a Mary Kay brochure in the waiting room. I said, "Wow! It's Mary Kay!"

The receptionist said, "Oh, do you use Mary Kay? We should call the lady." I called the number on the back of the brochure and made an appointment for her to come to our office for a complimentary facial and glamour makeover. Finding this consultant was a major turning point in my life, yet it happened by accident. How many times do we find opportunities where we least expect them, but yet how many go unnoticed as well?

I was excited to meet the Mary Kay beauty consultant and I encouraged a couple of my coworkers to join me for a facial at the office after work. The three of us agreed to get facials and glamour makeovers. I vividly remember how impressed I was by the way the beauty consultant's skin appeared. But more so, I noticed the way she applied her makeup. I thought I knew how to put on make-up. Was I wrong!

The woman must have thought I was silly, or maybe possessed, as I stared at her eye shadow and the way she blended her colors together. From her eye shadow, to her blush, to her lipstick, I was amazed at how she coordinated the colors together to compliment her skin tone and, even brought out the colors of her dress. She was attractive, and her ability to coordinate the beauty products with her overall appearance left a lifelong impression.

She taught us techniques for applying our make-up and showed the products that we should consider as part of our daily skin care and beauty regimen. I learned more techniques on how to apply eye shadow, as that was the most difficult to do. It involved balancing and coordinating colors and blending them to achieve a finished look. I kept thinking about how good she looked when this was done properly. For an hour every night for more than a week, I practiced at home in the bathroom until I was able to get the look that I was after.

Too shy, do not like sales, or talking to people I do not know

My Mary Kay beauty consultant called me several times and invited me to attend a Mary Kay meeting. She encouraged me to join as a beauty consultant. I responded that, even though I liked the products, *I was too shy, did not like sales, and did not like talking to people I do not know*. But, I went to the meetings anyway and just watched.

She continued to invite me to other glamour makeovers and meetings. After we had a glamour makeover at one session where they did the makeover on me, I received compliments on how I looked from others who attended. I was again encouraged to join as a beauty consultant. They told me that I was a *walking advertisement* for Mary Kay products. My reply, once again, was that *I was too shy, did not like sales, and did not like talking to people I do not know.*

That Christmas, I was shopping and a woman at the counter at Liberty House (now Macy's) gave me a compliment about my skin and makeup. I will always remember how proud and excited I was after I told her, "Thank you very much, I use Mary Kay skin care products."

She asked if I was a beauty consultant, and I replied, as usual, *I was too shy, did not like sales, and did not like talking to people I do not know*. At that moment, I realized I was starting to sound like a broken record. Plus, here I was talking to a person I did not know about how I was using and benefiting from Mary Kay products. It felt natural. Maybe I did not mind talking to people I did not know after all!

The kind woman recommended that I reconsider and become a beauty consultant. She said I was a "walking advertisement!" This was the second time that I had heard it put exactly that way. As I walked away, the words "walking advertisement" lingered in my mind.

I Wanted that Elegant Watch

Once again, I was invited to a Mary Kay meeting and was asked to be one of the models for the makeover session. My beauty consultant's sales director met with me and shared the Mary Kay marketing plan. I was still reluctant about the whole thing, because

I had convinced myself that *I was too shy, did not like sales, and did not like talking to people I do not know.*

When the sales director came to the house, I noticed a beautiful elegant watch on her wrist. I could not keep my eyes off that watch! It was the most elegant watch I had ever seen (in person or in a catalog). I asked her where she had bought it, as I had to buy one! She said that she did not buy it and they are not for sale; it was a prize from Mary Kay. I asked if I could buy the watch directly from Mary Kay. She said no. But, then she said if I were to join as a beauty consultant and recruit five new Mary Kay members, that I would get the same watch as a prize.

I wanted that elegant watch, so I joined Mary Kay. Suddenly, it did not matter that I thought *I was too shy, did not like sales, and did not like talking to people I do not know.* I went to the next meeting as the newest Mary Kay beauty consultant!

The *Newest Mary Kay Beauty Consultant*

As is routine at Mary Kay meetings, each beauty consultant stands and gives their name and summary of the sales for the week. They also give their progress towards winning a new car. I had no idea at my first meeting that I could win a car. I just wanted to win that elegant watch! I was impressed by the energy and confidence the women displayed at the meetings. I also was intrigued by the various members that were approaching the milestones for winning a new car. Some had the elegant watch, so I guess the car was next!

At that first meeting, I asked my sales director if I had to stand up and speak. She responded that yes, we have to do this. I told her I was shy. I had been telling her that for months, so surely she knew. But, when it was my turn to introduce myself, I had to speak to everyone! I thought, how could I do this? I told myself *I was too shy, did not like sales, and did not like talking to people I do not know.*

I was so nervous that my heart was racing. I got only as far as saying my name. I sat right back down, my knees still shaking. I thought I was going to faint! And, since I was new and did not have any sales totals to report, I figured, what more could I say? I started to wonder how badly I wanted that elegant watch. Doubts and fears crept in. But, I had gotten through my first meeting and that was no small thing for me at the time. I thought if I could do that much, maybe I could do more. I decided I needed to start selling product and signing up new customers. I wanted that elegant watch!

Persistency: Slow start but it pays off

When I became a Mary Kay beauty consultant, I invested over $700 for the Showcase and products to sell. That was a lot of money to take from my family savings account. But, I figured that with my mother, four sisters, and two female co-workers all placing orders, I would have a good start selling the products and getting closer to winning that elegant watch. At least, that was the plan.

I was not prepared for the negative reactions from my family. They scolded me and said that I should be spending more time with my family (my son was only a few months old), and not wasting time selling Mary Kay products and chasing silly dreams of success. They placed no orders---zero, nada. Every night I went to bed staring at the boxes of products I stacked in the bedroom. I remember wondering how I was going to sell all that product.

Despite those doubts, I kept reflecting on how good it felt when I received compliments on my skin and makeup, and how much I wanted to offer this experience to other women. I realized my instinct to do this was rooted in my wish to help others. I also remembered how much I wanted that elegant watch! Rather than listening to all the doubts and doubters, I chose to listen to my heart. It hurt, but I had to ignore all *naysayers*, especially those in my family.

Since my family refused to buy skin care products from me, I had no choice but to overcome my fear of talking to people I did not know. My first break came when one of my friends from the hospital agreed to have a facial on a weekend.

When giving the first facial, a new beauty consultant is supposed to have their sales director or someone else there to ensure everything goes well. I decided I could handle the facial on my own since I had so many of them done to me. I was nervous, but I figured that I could do the job well. Although I forgot some of the things we normally use during a facial, such as cotton balls, I *winged it* and my friend was happy with the colors I used to accentuate her skin tone. She bought the entire skin care and glamour set and was excited.

I was ecstatic! Not only did I close my first sale, but I felt that I made a difference in her appearance and her attitude. I had helped her! She was so happy with the results that she introduced me to her mother, who also bought a product set. Now, the *light bulb* in my head really came on and I came to believe that I could do this. And, it was not just from a sales point of view, but from a deep-seated wish to help, to share, to educate, and to develop the best in my fellow women.

I was so enthusiastic about the impact of what I did that I nearly forgot about the elegant watch that I wanted so badly. The experience that I had with those two women was a turning point in my mind-set and attitude towards the Mary Kay program. The change of perspective from the watch to helping others was more important, as was my new-found self-confidence. The watch was what I originally wanted---and, I did get it---but I ended up with far more! I realized *I was NOT too shy, DID like sales, and DID like talking to people I do not know.*

Mary Kay Team Leader and Car

After several years of continued success giving facials and selling product, my sales director, Perlita Ancheta, asked me why I was not sharing the opportunity and enrolling other beauty consultants. My response was that I was more interested in giving the facials and in the side income. I also said that I did not quite understand the benefits of bringing in other beauty consultants.

I told my sales director that I was not sure how to explain the marketing plan and that I did not want to lose them as paying clients. Perlita stressed that by recruiting other women, I would be helping to open the doors of opportunity for these women much as she had done for me. They would be able to get discounts on the products and to also grow personally and professionally.

The advice resonated, as I recalled my first two sales when I was more thrilled with bringing something positive into those women's lives than in making a few dollars. My sales director challenged me to become a Team Leader. That meant I had to recruit and train three new beauty consultants. A Team Leader has the privilege of wearing a special Mary Kay red jacket at meetings.

The Mary Kay system sets a high priority on rewarding those who achieve positive results. I enjoyed the recognition, prizes, and rewards that I received at the weekly meetings. When my sales director outlined a path for me to recruit three beauty consultants so that I could earn Team Leader status, I set my goal on that achievement. I also learned that if I found five new beauty consultants that would make me eligible to win a new Mary Kay car!

One of our friends from church was a Mary Kay beauty consultant and she drove a new Mary Kay car. When I saw her driving, I would imagine a new Mary Kay car in our garage. I wanted a second car for the family, but we could not afford another car payment and insurance. It was then that I realized that with continued encouragement from my sales director, I could achieve even higher levels of success with Mary Kay and this success would benefit my entire family!

In 1995, my sales director invited me to a Mary Kay convention in Dallas. I was concerned about the cost of attending the convention and wondered if the expense was worth it. My friend, Timi Torcato, who brought me into the company, also encouraged me to attend so I could see the *big picture* of the Mary Kay Company. After discussing it with my family, I went to the convention. I was amazed being in the presence of over 10,000 other Mary Kay women. The convention atmosphere was overwhelming! Everyone was friendly and open with hospitality. I vividly recall the positive energy and the beautiful appearance of each woman.

I knew I made the correct choice to attend my first Mary Kay convention! There were dynamic sessions where women gave speeches and testimonials about their journeys and success. Many awards were given in recognition of success levels achieved. The winners went up on a huge stage for all to see and share in the celebration. At first I thought it was odd that these women were applauding competing sales consultants. But, I realized this was a team of people working together, not against one another.

I also remember hearing from some of the Senior, Executive, and National Sales Directors who were earning large sums of money every month from their involvement in Mary Kay. There were two National Sales Directors who were in their sixties and were about to retire. They said that their retirement income was over $58,000. At first I thought that was not much for a year, but I soon found out that it was $58,000 a month, not a year! I was amazed. These women were beautiful, well-dressed, confident, and they were rich! I decided that I wanted to be like them and be able to retire with no wrinkles or sagging skin and with such a nice income. My goodness, how far I had come from merely seeking one watch as a reward!

I was aware of the hard work and sacrifice that these women had to endure to achieve their levels of success. Knowing this, I was all the more impressed by them because of their attitude, their graciousness, and their enthusiasm towards the Mary Kay program, as well as their concern for me and my future success.

The Mary Kay Black Suit with Gold Trim

During the sales seminar at the convention, I noticed several women wearing beautifully-tailored black suits with gold trimming. I asked my sales director how I could get into one of those suits. She told me that was the 'Director's Suit' and I would need to qualify by having thirty qualified beauty consultants within four months.

I was even more impressed by those who were being recognized and applauded as the *Queen's Court of Sales, Court of Recruiting*, who were the directors who received their new Mary Kay pink cars. It was at that moment I told myself that I wanted to be onstage next year when I came back to attend the seminar!

Mary Kay had written a book *You Can Have It All* that was being sold at the convention. I waited in line for a very long time to buy two copies. The convention events finished at midnight on the third day and I had little time to sleep before a 4:00 a.m. departure to return home to Hawaii. Even with only two hours sleep, I was energized on my long journey home. On the flight back, I read the entire book. I pictured myself in the beautiful black director's suit at next year's convention and I visualized myself on stage in the Queen's Court of Recruiting!

Back at Home - Making Impossible Possible

My sales director told me that it normally takes four months to achieve the director's position. She noted that to earn the position I had to have thirty qualified beauty consultants and at least $32,000 in retail product orders from the company. I told her that I was going to do this in one month! She said that was impossible. This had never been done before in Hawaii and was rarely done nationally. She literally could not believe what I had said. At the time, I was working full-time at one hospital and part-time at another. I also had two small children to take care of while my husband was away on a business trip.

The very next day, I started to earn the director's position. After my day at the hospital, I would focus on recruiting women and training them. I would take my three-year old daughter with me who often fell asleep in the backseat of the car on our way home. I remember carrying her upstairs to sleep and being very tired. But, I had faith that all this work would soon pay off for us. I told myself, "I can do this" as I imagined wearing the black director's suit!

Halfway through the month, I questioned myself, wondering how in the world I could carry this out in one month. At this point, I was almost halfway to my goal. I recall looking into the mirror every morning, pointing a finger at myself, and insisting, "You can do it!" I remained focused and positive, even though at times I would answer myself with, "Are you nuts?" As I found in every aspect of my life, if I had a positive attitude, I could succeed more than anyone ever thought possible.

Of course, I ought to mention that I did not do this alone. All the beauty consultants in my unit worked together as a team and were as excited as I was about achieving this goal. One who put forth special effort, and to whom I am very grateful, is Tessie Pascua. I went with her and another beauty consultant to the outer islands at least three times that month. We sold about $3,000 each weekend, working until midnight. Then, to reward ourselves, we would go dancing!

My recruiter, Timi Torcato, constantly met with me in the afternoons after work and monitored our production, calculating how much more I needed to qualify for director that month.

A major inspiration for me during those trying times was a popular song by Helen Reddy: *I Am Woman*. I would play that song over and over in my car. My daughter Jessica was in preschool at the time, and she knew all the words to the song and would sing along.

"I am woman, hear me roar..."
"Yes, I've paid the price, but look how much I've gained..."
"You can bend but never break me

'Cause it only serves to make me
More determined to achieve my final goal
And I come back even stronger
Not a novice any longer
'Cause you've deepened the conviction in my soul..."

I would also constantly pray to God to help me with my goals. I was always proud that Mary Kay, as part of the company's business philosophy, reinforces *God first, family second, career third.* It helped me learn how to balance everything pretty well, all things considered.

And, after thirty days---Hallelujah!!!---I broke the record for the State of Hawaii: I qualified for the directorship in the shortest time ever, making the impossible possible and earning the right to wear that beautiful black jacket.

CHAPTER 4

The Impact Of Mary Kay: Living The American Dream

Joni believes: "Dreams do come true."

"Delight yourself in the LORD and
He will give you the desires of your heart."
Psalm 37:4 (NIV)

Meeting Mary Kay, my mentor

After the excitement of the annual Mary Kay convention that recognized the top performers and sales directors, and after reading Mary Kay's book "You Can Have It All" on the flight home, I knew I just had to meet the woman responsible for all this. I wanted to have the opportunity to see the woman who was quickly becoming my idol. I also felt deeply that I wanted to thank her for being the inspiration that changed my life. This was my new goal! Suddenly my prior goal of winning that elegant watch was but a stepping-stone. I set my sights on meeting Mary Kay.

On my return home after the convention, I began my plan to become a Director in Mary Kay. During my Mary Kay directorship qualifications, I was encouraged to qualify a total of fifty Mary Kay Beauty Consultants. When you achieved the "Elite Fabulous Fifty" milestone, you were qualified to have lunch with Mary Kay in a private dining room. Since my new goal was to meet Mary Kay---and SOON---I was going to get twenty new Beauty Consultants to add to my current thirty, for a total of fifty, as quickly as I possibly could.

Mary Kay had become a distant mentor and personal hero to me as well as to many others. Her philosophy of life was *God first, family second, career third.* Her ability to reach out and make a difference to so many inspired me to want to be a better person. Mary Kay and her business helped to change the lives of many women; certainly she helped to make me and my life better. Though she did not know me, Mary Kay helped me develop myself despite any self-perceived flaws that I had about my size, shape, ethnicity, color, shyness, or any other area I had self-doubts about. Being part of the Mary Kay business gave me the tools to learn to believe in myself.

Suddenly, I realized I had confidence and believed that I could achieve any goal I set by applying focused hard work. The Mary Kay experience gave me the courage to dream and follow my dreams. I learned the value of focus. From reading Mary Kay's book and from hearing the many stories, I decided that if she could achieve her goals, so could I. After all, I had her as my inspiration. I often wondered if Mary Kay had such an "inspiration" who gave her hope and motivation as she did for me. I was going to ask her when we met!

It was my longtime dream to meet Mary Kay in person and to have a conversation with her. This dream kept me motivated despite the long hours, hard work, and juggling my precious family and my nursing career. I was going to see my dream come true! I closed in on my goal of becoming a member of the Elite Fabulous Fifty. Moving from twenty to thirty and then onto fifty new beauty consultants become easier and easier as I had learned how to manage my Mary Kay business. I also earned a reputation for helping those I enrolled. Soon, I was doing well in my own business but also helping others to be successful. I started to understand what some call "karma," where one gets as much as they give.

I was living a busy life with a full schedule. I was working full-time at one hospital and part-time at another. I also had my family and two children who at the time were nine and three years old. I was working my Mary Kay business part-time. I thought getting into the Elite Fabulous Fifty was going to take longer than I wanted it to, but I needed to keep my life in perspective and keep a healthy family environment. Much like Mary Kay's philosophy: *God first, family second, career third.*

Teamwork

Up to this point in my Mary Kay career, I was a Team Manager working mostly on my own, but meeting others at regular meetings. When I started to aim for the Elite Fabulous Fifty, a friend who was also a beauty consultant was trying to qualify as well. What worked well for us both is that we began helping and challenging each other. It was then that I learned the value of teamwork and working with colleagues, not in competition, but in a spirit of cooperation to help each other succeed.

Having a friend and colleague provided a competitive spirit that helped us both achieve our goals faster than we could have otherwise. This was a great inspiration as I worked much harder and at the end of one month, I had met the qualifications. Over the last twenty-five years in Hawaii, no one had qualified in one month; I set a new record! I wanted to meet Mary Kay with my friend who had not yet achieved the fifty total beauty consultants. I encouraged her and told her I would wait one month so we could meet Mary Kay together.

At the end of the third month, my friend still did not qualify. I told her that I would have to go ahead as I could no longer wait for the chance to meet Mary Kay. I had considered waiting another month or two as it was normally a four-month period that most took to get qualified, but I did it in one month and I wanted to meet Mary Kay.

Meeting Mary Kay

I was qualified and it was driving me nuts to not be on my way to meet Mary Kay. I was so excited; I wanted to go the next day after I qualified with my fiftieth beauty consultant. It took four very long weeks from the time I qualified until I could attend the next scheduled event. Every day I woke up and practiced what questions I would ask.

I was so excited to have achieved this milestone. All I could think about was getting on a plane and flying from Honolulu to Dallas to meet Mary Kay, as part the new director's training program. When I finally did met Mary Kay, I was thrilled to see, hug, and touch her. How often does one get to meet their mentor whom they had heard so much about? I knew this day was going to be one of the highlights of my life---and, it was!

I had tears in my eyes when I arrived before meeting Mary Kay. And then suddenly for a short period of time, it felt like the carpet was pulled right out from under me when I heard that of the 285 new sales directors, only ten were going to meet Mary Kay personally. I was shocked and disappointed at first, until I learned that I was one of those ten. While I was happy, I could not help but wonder how many others had similar dreams that would not be fulfilled. I sensed that my hard work and getting fifty beauty consultants enrolled in record time helped me to be chosen. Maybe "karma" was returning the good deeds I had done earlier.

When I finally met Mary Kay, a day I will remember forever, she was larger than life, but yet friendly and down to earth. She had a way of making me feel important and special. Mary Kay asked me several questions while looking me straight in the eyes. She was interested in what I had to say. This made me feel even more drawn to her; she showed that she was caring and giving. It was obvious that she wanted to enrich our lives during this special meeting.

When we were having pictures taken together, I noticed that we were about the same height – meaning short. I mentioned this and Mary Kay responded, "No, Joni, we are petite!" I have not been short since that day! While we shared an hour together, it seemed longer but at the same time it ended all too soon. I could have spent the entire day with her.

The Last Batch

As it happened, it was a good thing I did not wait any longer to meet Mary Kay. The month I met Mary Kay was to be the last month that she could meet new directors. Shortly afterwards, she suffered a stroke. When I heard that Mary Kay had a stroke, I was devastated. But, at the same time, I felt honored to have had the opportunity to have met her, knowing I was in the "last batch" of Elite Fabulous Fifty that had that opportunity. My friend, who qualified in four months, was not able to meet Mary Kay as I had. I felt that God had heard my prayers and ensured I would meet Mary Kay and thus it happened.

As I looked back on the time I was focused on meeting Mary Kay, I gained far more than the honor of meeting my mentor. I believed I learned valuable life lessons from setting a goal, helping those I brought into the business, and teamwork. One of the most valuable lessons I learned from my association with the Mary Kay business that still is carried with me today is courage: the courage to realize and work toward fulfilling my dreams. The Mary Kay business may consist of many independent beauty consultants, but those that are successful are anything but on their own.

Attitude Measures Altitude

People often ask how I can do so much while appearing refreshed. They ask, "Do you ever sleep?" and "Where do you get your energy?" and "Where do you find time to do all that you do?" I always tell them, "By having a *Million Dollar Attitude!*"

I believe that our attitude measures our altitude. I also tell them that I learned from Mary Kay how to prioritize, organize, and balance my time. Plus, I can honestly say "Because I have been a good girl, God blessed me by giving me six more hours in a day!"

If not for Mary Kay, I would not have achieved the success that I have today. The positive impact of Mary Kay on my life has revealed itself in many ways. It started from using the basic Mary Kay skin care products that resulted in an improvement in my complexion. That, in turn, gave me self-confidence from the compliments I received on my appearance. Later, I received encouragement and recognition for the business success I was achieving. Finally, through Mary Kay, I gained a sense of how people develop relationships that comfort and bring importance to one's life. The *Million Dollar Attitude* is a result of all my experience and is my guiding philosophy as well.

Freedom from a Job

When my son Jason and daughter Jessica were young, I was working in the medical field full-time at one hospital and part-time at another, and simply did not have the time to attend my children's school events. From Mary Kay, I learned I could create the work and family balance that I so much wanted. As my success increased in the cosmetic industry, I was rewarded well for my hard work. My ability to plan and organize my time paid big dividends via increased sales and commissions.

I was driving a red car with automobile insurance that was provided to me free by Mary Kay. I also had built up my business with Mary Kay to the point that I found the courage to leave my full-time nursing position to be able to spend more time with my family. Leaving the salaried nursing position for the commission-based Mary Kay business was a bit scary; but everything soon fell into place. My self-confidence, and the income, allowed me to make that important decision. Mary Kay not only provided a car for me to drive, but was the vehicle to allow me to live the *American Dream* of having my own business with the flexibility to work around my family time.

Having the freedom to set my own schedule turned out to be a blessing when my mother was diagnosed with a brain tumor. She needed someone to help during the emotionally and physically difficult pre- and post-surgery times. I was fortunate that I could make the time. My sisters had full-time jobs and did not have the flexibility to help out. My younger sister, Nikky Leahey, who lived in Boston, took off from work, but she had to return home after two weeks. I picked up Mom's medication and took her to the doctor for follow-up and treatments. At other times, I was there just to add comfort and be with her during her difficult time.

There was no way I could have done all that if I had a full-time job. One time when we were driving home from a doctor's appointment, I reminded Mom of the times she used to scold me about my work in Mary Kay.

"Mother," I said, "Do you realize you are riding in my free Mary Kay pink car?"

I pointed out to her that if I had quit Mary Kay, like she told me to back then, I would not have the luxury of taking her to her appointments.

I remember one Thanksgiving morning when I got up early to put the turkey in the oven so I could go do a couple of facials. That was the only time my clients could do it. They worked, too! My mother called while I was giving those facials and educating the women to look good and feel good about them. She was upset and raised her voice to me. She wanted to know where I was and what I was doing. I told her I was with my Mary Kay clients. My mother did not understand nor recognize my work with Mary Kay then. During that call, she actually accused me of cheating on my husband! Oh, my goodness! After all the hard work I had put into Mary Kay and the great rewards I earned and shared with my family, I was hurt. My mother did not believe me.

That was a long time ago and my mother eventually came to realize that my hard work was to make things better for my family.

Years later, my mother told me she was worried about me driving for my Mary Kay business, especially late at night, because my older sister Lu was killed in a car accident at the age of thirty-three. This was tragic for the family, especially since the accident happened on Mother's Day. I am glad I did not let her fears derail my career path, though, because the success that she was so opposed to ended up giving us precious time together.

CHAPTER 5
Cosmetics To Insurance

Joni believes: "The road to success
is always under construction."

"Commit to the LORD whatever you do,
and your plans will succeed."
Proverbs 16:3 (NIV)

Family Tragedy Inspires

I was inspired to get into the insurance business when two tragic family experiences influenced my life deeply. My sister Lu passed away because of a car accident. For me, this was simply devastating. My sister and I were as close as twins. She was more than a sister; she was my best friend. We did so many things together. We would go dancing, to the beach, to the movies, and to parties.

Three months before the fatal car accident, a friend had tried to sell my sister life insurance. She did not buy it, saying, "I am single, have no dependents, no husband, and still live with my parents. So, I don't need life insurance. What for?"

The insurance agent did not fully explain to my sister the various types of insurance. Thus, my sister assumed that all life insurance policies were *term-life*, which provides only temporary benefits. She did not know that with a *whole-life* insurance policy, you and your family have benefits whether you die prematurely or live a long time. My parents wanted to give Lu the best funeral service possible, since this was the last thing that they could do for her. They spent almost $20,000 for her funeral. And, because there was no insurance, my parents paid for the funeral from their retirement fund.

This tragic experience of both losing my sister and seeing my parent's retirement money spent affected me deeply. I was mad at my sister for passing away and I was mad at the insurance agent who could have clearly told my sister about the value of different types of insurance programs. Because of this, I gained a passionate need to learn more myself and to then educate others about the importance of planning to ensure that they and their loved ones are protected from financial hardship should a tragic event occur.

Another tragic experience hit close to home. My older sister, Leriza Godoy, had twin sons, one of whom got malignant brain cancer at the age of three. He required surgery. My sister had taken out $25,000 of insurance on the twins when they were one year old, so this served to keep the family's finances from disastrous consequences.

Twelve years later, the brain cancer reoccurred, this time in an aggressive form. Chemotherapy, radiation, and four surgeries could not stop the malignancy. Because of my medical background, my sister asked for my help. And, again, because of my flexible work hours, I could help. Although the doctors did all they could, my nephew passed away from the disease. While this was devastating to the family, there was some comfort in that the insurance policy my sister had taken out many years ago served them well and kept this from becoming a financial tragedy as well. This experience further reinforced my belief that the right type of life insurance is something of great value to people and their families. You never know when you may need it, and this provides great comfort and peace of mind.

Hello Insurance Industry

From this I was motivated to consider getting into the insurance industry and taking my insurance license exam. I shared my thoughts with a friend who was already licensed in life, health, and other insurance products. He discouraged me from pursuing my ambitions in this area. He told me the insurance business is one of the worst to be in, from an income point of view, adding that he had a difficult time selling life insurance policies, even to friends and family.

While I listened to my friend's advice, I more so heard my instincts, my inner voice, that reminded me of the lessons I had learned from my family's experience. I felt I had done well in sales with Mary Kay and I was aware of the great sense of well-being that came from helping others. While I heard the voice of my friend and considered his input, I had to listen to my own inner voice. I would not be discouraged from going into the insurance industry.

Getting Licensed: Not So Easy

To achieve my goal, I needed to first learn about the insurance industry. I took the initiative by taking classes to become familiar with the industry terminology and the laws of the insurance industry. The class was also part of my preparation to take the licensing exams for life and health insurance.

After a short period of time studying, I thought that I knew enough to take the exam. I quickly learned how little I knew when I earned 51% and 53% on each exam (70% was passing). I was disappointed with my performance. This was the first time I failed in something I wanted badly. While this was difficult to accept, I believed that God was telling me *not to give up.*

With my *Million Dollar Attitude*, I enrolled in another insurance class in a different school. This new school had a nontraditional approach. This school did not use books and there was no writing. The only method of learning was through interaction with one another. A bit skeptical, I attended the classes and "interacted." At the time, I was more comfortable with conventional learning methods. But, I decided to be open to new ways of learning. Much as with Mary Kay, I had to trust the system.

I remember that once in a while, I would take a pen and write the relevant information onto my hand – much like a young schoolchild. Then, I would sneak out to the women's room and write the "kernel of wisdom" onto a napkin so I could study it later. Well, despite my tenacious study habits, including the covert women's room transcriptions, on my second try at the exam, I earned only 57 and 58%. But, hey, I did better!

If at First You Do Not Succeed

After I failed the exam a second time, I noticed a job advertisement posted in the local newspaper by a well-known insurance company. I called them and asked if applicants needed a license to work for them. The receptionist said no. Without hesitation, I said I would like to apply for the job and requested an interview. I was going to learn the insurance business and help people after all!

When I arrived for my interview a few days later, I met with one of the managers. He educated me about their employee benefits program and asked me if I knew at least fifty people. I chuckled as I thought of my Mary Kay client list and the people I knew in the cosmetic industry. "Yes," I said, "I know many more than fifty people."

The manager gave me a form to fill out. I had to provide a list of the people and their basic contact information. I completed the list and gave it to him. I was feeling confident about the interview. I thought I responded well to the questions that were asked. I was getting excited about this new opportunity until the manager mentioned that eventually I would have to get an insurance license. What? I told the manager that when I called to set up this interview, the receptionist told me that a license was not needed. Unfortunately, she was wrong and I would not be able to sell life insurance without the license.

I was ashamed to confess to the manager that I had already had tried to pass the exam twice, without success. I said I was getting weary of paying the $75 exam fee! Then, suddenly, the manager's boss from an adjacent room blurted out that "the $75 will come back tenfold." He made it sound easy, but at the time, it seemed like a lot to me.

After that blow, I picked myself up off the floor and decided to go for it again. The manager promised that he would help me study and prepare for the next exam. In the meanwhile, he would permit me to make appointments to discuss policies with potential clients. During this period, I was effectively acting as an intern, with the manager supervising me. He came with me to appointments and took the responsibility for all applications.

My manager was amazed that at every appointment that I arranged, I would not only make the sale, but the clients, more than once, would give me a signed blank check with no date or amount. He was obviously impressed, not only with my sales expertise, but even more by the way that these clients would simply trust me with what I told them. Blank checks? Unbelievable! I do not think he had ever seen that before. That was okay, I had never seen it before, either!

Third Time is a Charm. Or is it?

The manager had high hopes for me passing the exam on my third try. So did I! I studied and believed I was better prepared to take the exam the third time. I approached the exam with confidence hoping that I would prevail. After all, the third time is a charm. But, again to my dismay, I did not pass with 70% or better. I achieved only 63% and 65% on the exams.

Even though my scores improved, I was so disappointed. Truthfully, I thought about giving up. But, quitting is not something that I have ever been comfortable with. I kept thinking of a saying I heard years ago: *Quitters never win, and winners never quit.*

I was not sure how to approach the manager and tell him that I did not pass. I was right to be anxious, as he had a negative reaction to the bad news. We already had a stack of about twenty applications that could not be submitted unless I passed the exam. My manager was more than ready for me to get my license and sign all those applications. While he was upset at my failure, he was impressed with my people skills enough that he was not ready to give up on me.

I Am No Quitter!

My manager's message to me was clear: this time, study day and night and pass the test! Believe me, I studied day and night. The night before I was to take the exam for the fourth time, I was lying on the couch and studying. I was wearing a comfortable aloha dress. I was so comfortable that I fell asleep and woke up the next morning later than I would have liked. If I was to make it to the exam on time, I could not waste time changing my outfit. I drove as fast as I could to town for the exam. I realized that this would be the first time that I ever wore the same outfit two days in a row. I was thinking that this might bring me some good luck and break the "spell." After all, the fourth time is a charm, or so that day I was praying.

I barely arrived on time and took the exam. Once again, I was anxious. More so because of the pressure from my manager to "pass or else." I was not as confident as I had been the other times. Perhaps the fear of failure was starting to get to me!

While taking the exam, I carefully read and then reread the questions. When I was done answering all the questions, I went back over the exam yet again to make sure that I had gotten as many correct answers as possible. I was sweating it out, big time! I took a deep breath and looked up. I saw that I was the only one left in the room! Everyone else had finished.

When I handed in the answer sheets, the proctor graded the exam right then and there. I do not believe they wanted to see me there a fifth time any more than I wanted to be there again! I was nervous while waiting for the results that would decide my fate. I was pacing back and forth, worrying, sweating, expectant, heart pounding while waiting for the verdict. Finally, the clerk called me, saying simply, "You passed."

I was so relieved! I was happy, excited, and jumping for joy, all at the same time. I was so happy, I almost forgot to ask for my score. Given the huge amount of time I studied for all these exams, I was expecting to maybe get a 95%. That would be about right.

She looked up and said, "Seventy-one percent on both life and health. You made it, barely." This did not detract from my joyous state. I passed!

I rushed to the office to share the great news with my manager. I screamed that I passed both the life and health parts of the exam. I told him, "I have a pen and I am ready and able to sign those applications!" He had me sign the waiting applications immediately. I was simply ecstatic from passing the test. Now my manager, who believed in me, could be paid based on the applications I was able to secure.

Life Lesson

There was a good life lesson for me in how long it took me to pass the exams. I found out that I had a drive and commitment to my goals. It would have been easy for me to quit after any of the first three tries. In fact, many of my close friends encouraged me to quit as they did not think that I had it in me to be an insurance salesperson. I realized they were trying to help me feel better. But, I never would have quit if I did not successfully pass that exam whether it was the fourth time or the fourteenth. It was a goal and I saw it through. No one could take that away from me! *Quitters never win, and winners never quit.*

Success in New Ways

Once I earned the elusive license and heard the "Atta girl" from my manager, I was off and running. In my second month, I was the top producer of the month for Hawaii and was the insurance company's Number One salesperson. By the third month, I was the winner of the Fast Start award for new agents.

From that point, I was normally the top producer every month and after completing my first year, I was able to qualify for the Million Dollar Roundtable (MDRT) recognition. At the time, I did not know the significance of the bestowed recognition. I learned that this honor was reserved for the country's top two percent of registered insurance agents, based on production, commissions, and number of clients. My manager also mentioned that I could become the "Rookie of the Year" and "Top Producer" of the year---and, I did! I started to sense that the insurance industry, much like Mary Kay, had many levels of qualifications to help provide positive feedback and incentives to help sale people be recognized for their hard work.

I traveled to New Orleans for the Million Dollar Roundtable convention. There were 61 countries represented and about 7,000 MDRT top producers in attendance. At this convention, some people were curious about me. My nametag showed I was from Hawaii and that I had written 228 "lives" which is what we called policies that had been approved and delivered.

I was asked, "How did you get 228 lives in only one year?" They'd also ask, "How many years have you been in the insurance industry?"

When I told them I had been in only one year, they were shocked. Most of them had been in insurance for 10, 15, or even 20 years, with many of them making the MDRT for the first time.

The next big question was, "How did you do it?"

I told them I was Wonder Woman! Actually, I told them I was a Mary Kay sales director and that I not only got many of my clients from my Mary Kay business, but that Mary Kay had taught me how to network, how to approach people, and how to prioritize my time. I added that my family experiences had given me a passion for educating people and helping them to make good decisions regarding their financial security. I had seen what can happen when people do not plan ahead for the future.

Some of the MDRT producers, even the men, replied that maybe they should join Mary Kay!

Trouble on the Horizon

I was enjoying my newfound professional status. While I was selling insurance I also actively recruited new agents into the company. One day, I received a call from a friend who was also in the insurance industry. He was getting ready for a second interview with a rival company. He asked me to go with him. My friend simply wanted a second opinion, since I was doing well in the business. I agreed to go along and listen, watch, and perhaps offer my thoughts.

During the interview, the General Agent of the rival company showed interest in me, asking me questions about my background. He was curious about how I achieved the Million Dollar Roundtable after only one year. I did not share anything specific other than I was blessed and fortunate to be able to work for a good company that treated me well. I also said that my *Million Dollar Attitude* was essential to my organizing and time management skills.

I could not help but be impressed with this rival company's employee benefit package as well as with the products the company offered. This rival company seemed to offer more flexibility, more time freedom, and more autonomy to its insurance agents than I was enjoying. What struck me the most was that their insurance products were better designed to meet the client's needs. While personnel benefits are important, their insurance programs seemed to be designed more so to serve the many needs of those who want and need insurance.

When I went back to my office, I shared this information with some of the agents that I had recruited, and many of them found it all too hard to believe. Many said, "Too good to be true!" They asked me to set up an appointment with the General Agent from the rival company so they could hear it for themselves. A couple of days later, on a Friday, a few of them went to listen to the General Agent of the other company to learn more.

Over the weekend, a friend that I had recruited called to ask if I was going to move to the other rival company. I told her that I was going to talk with our manager to discuss what I learned and to gain his feedback. Our manager was on a business trip and not due back until Monday of the next week. I asked that she not bring this up with our manager or anyone else until I had a chance to discuss it with him first.

My manager arrived Monday evening, and little did I know that my so-called "friend" had called him that evening at home. She asked about the other company and told him of my discussions with the rival General Agent the week before. When I went to work on Tuesday, I planned to meet with my manager and ask his opinion of the other company. That morning, I received a telephone call from one of the agents that I had brought into the company. She warned me that "something was up." She explained the manager told all agents there would be an emergency meeting, and she suspected that someone had told him of our visiting the other company.

I could not imagine that my other friend would have gone behind my back when I specifically asked her to let me bring this issue to our manager myself. I called another agent, asking if she was the one that spoke to our manager, and she said no. I knew who it was. It was my friend, and I immediately called her and asked what she had told the manager. She replied innocently that she only called to wish him a happy birthday, and casually asked what he knew about the other company.

When I stepped into my office, I was shocked to see that all my client's files were gone. I had a bad feeling, and went to my manager's office. I noticed he was standing by his office doorway, glaring at me. I returned his glare, noting that I was upset that my files would have been confiscated without talking with me first.

When I asked him where my files were, he replied that he took them away. We went into his office and he talked at me and did not listen to what I had to say. He accused me of being disloyal to the company and was upset because he had helped me so much. He did not seem to realize that I did all the hard work to bring in so much business. Then, he took me to the 17th floor to the Vice President's office. I thought I would be able to share that I did not say I would go work for another company, but he still wouldn't listen to me.

Once in the Vice President's office, he and two other men accused me of signing a contract to go to work with the rival company. I told them I did not sign anything and I was only listening to what they had to say. I told them I was going to speak to my manager when he returned today to get his insights on what I learned and heard. They would not listen to me either. They gave me a termination letter that was already typed and signed. They warned me not to try to transfer any of my clients.

My manager went on to talk down the other company, adding the General Agent there had been known to make false promises. Basically, my manager was afraid of losing salespeople and clients to the rival company. I went to my office and started to pack my personal belongings. The manager helped me, with a push-cart no less, so he could get me out of the office as fast as possible.

As I was packing, my friend who had spoken out of turn, dropped in saying, "Oh, you're packing?" I responded, "Yes, thanks to you!"

Making Lemonade from Lemons

Later, I called the General Agent of the rival company and told him of the drama that had taken place. He felt bad and said, "Come over." When I arrived, I found a beautiful arrangement of a dozen long stem red roses.

The General Agent asked me what had happened, so I explained everything that went on. He was incredulous. "How could they do this to you?" he said. "You have been their top producer."

I told him that they had accused me of signing a contract here at this office, with no basis, and terminated me without even listening to me. The General Agent asked me what my plans were. I responded, "When do I start here? Since I no longer have a job, do you want to hire me?"

He told me to come back the next day and that a contract would be ready for me. He made me feel better, especially when I realized I had not even filled out an application and he was willing to hire me on the spot!

After I moved, I contacted my prior clients, advising them that I was with a different company. I gave them a choice and asked if they still wanted me to be their financial representative. Most responded that they bought the prior policy because of me, and because of their trust in me. They were disappointed and felt bad for me because they knew how hard I had worked for the company and how committed I was to providing the best service to my clients.

Overwhelmingly, they trusted me and elected to stay with me. I heard later, from many of my clients and from former agents, that my prior company had reassigned my roughly 400 clients to five different agents. I heard that some of these agents advised my clients not to listen to me, that I was terminated, got fired, and that I should not be trusted. Little did these agents know that I had known these clients over a long period time---some for fifteen to twenty years. Many were friends; not just clients.

I am sure it came as a shock to these agents that no matter what they said to my clients and friends, they were not able to keep them. My clients simply trusted me, not the company. Many of my clients wrote letters to the President of the company, stating their displeasure with the way I was treated and the unprofessional manner with which the situation was handled.

Within six months, I was pleased to find that I was ranked #1 statewide, and #2 nationwide, with my new company, Guardian Life Insurance Company of America. With God's help, and with hard work, dedication, and commitment, I was able to work through this difficult transition and once again be successful. Having an excellent line of products to share, and most importantly, having the personal motivation to help others that grew out of my family experiences, helped, too. I noted again how attitude and outlook affect situations. My *Million Dollar Attitude* was becoming a hallmark of my work ethic and was resulting in great personal and financial rewards.

At Guardian Life, I was consistently recognized and rewarded for obtaining clients, writing policies, and sharing the career opportunity with potential new agents. I was promoted to Career Development Supervisor after one year with the company.

Like Mary Kay, Guardian Life believes in recognizing its leaders. After my first year with Guardian Life, I received the following awards:

Leaders Club
Centurion Club
Presidential Citation Award
for Outstanding Achievement in Field Management
National Sales Achievement Award
National Quality Award
Million Dollar Round Table

That same year, 2002, I was honored with the U.S. SBA Women in Business Advocate of the Year Award. I was nominated by Bill Rol of Bank of Hawaii. He was impressed with my energy and entrepreneurial spirit, and the fact that, through my work at Guardian Life and Mary Kay Cosmetics, I was in a position to inspire other women to follow their dreams into business ownership, new careers and more fulfilling lives. He also recognized my efforts in serving in a variety of community service organizations. I'm very proud of this award. The ceremony was held at the Sheraton Hotel and 500 or more people were in attendance. This made it very special for me, especially when I thought back on my humble beginnings.

From August to December 2005, after only six years with Guardian Life, I qualified as the #1 Life Application producer nationwide. I was number one out of thousands of Financial Representatives. This accomplishment was particularly satisfying for me because that year I had a lot on my plate, as you'll read about in later chapters. My General Agent, Gary Gragson, constantly encouraged me, saying, "You will be Number One!" He even introduced me to people as "Number One" before it happened. It stuck in my mind that I had to do it!

I prayed and prayed and kept reading my inspirational poems. December is normally the slowest month in the insurance industry because people are busy shopping and partying. But, that did not stop me; I kept going. I turned in 55 insurance applications that month and 51 of them were paid and delivered. The average for the industry is around 25 to 30 policies per agent per year.

Again, my habit of visualizing results paid off. Earlier that year, in June 2005, Gary gave me a list of the Top 50 agents in the company, ranked by policies written. At that time, I was Number Four. I took the list and crossed out the name of whoever was Number One and wrote in my name. I also wrote in my target number of policies for December as 50 and my year-to-date total goal as 200. I kept this "revised" list with me and looked at it often. At the end of the year, the actual figures were 51 policies for December and 208 policies for the entire year.

THE ROAD TO SUCCESS

The Road to Success is NOT straight.
There is a Curve called…FAILURE
A Loop called…CONFUSION
Speed Bumps called…FRIENDS
Red Lights called…ENEMIES
Caution Lights called…FAMILY
You will have Flats called…JOBS.

BUT

If you have a Spare called…DETERMINATION
An Engine called…PERSERVERANCE
Insurance called…FAITH
A Chauffeur called…JESUS
You will make it to a Place called SUCCESS!

Author Unknown

CHAPTER 6
Don't Get Tired Of Doing What Is Right

Joni believes: "Be rich in kindness
and slow to anger."

"But as for you, be strong and do not
give up, for your work will be rewarded."
2 Chronicles 15:7

Nominated for Entrepreneur of the Year

Zeny Muyot, a part-time announcer at KNDI radio station, heard about me and my success with Mary Kay and with the insurance industry. At the time, we attended the same church but did not know each other. Zeny was active in the Filipino community on Oahu, Hawaii. She contacted me and then we met. After our meeting, she invited me to the radio station to be interviewed.

I was surprised to be invited for an interview. Why would she want to interview me? It was a half hour radio show and I was the guest for the entire session. She asked questions about my career, my family, and how I balanced such a busy schedule. I answered her questions and I read one of my favorite poems on the air. I had read it to Zeny earlier and she also found it inspirational. It begins

"Lord, I need to be a winner, not for me, but for You.
People are watching and I am the example they will follow...."

For me, this poem is inspirational as it speaks to my heartfelt wish to be the example that others can follow. Zeny and her producer must have been impressed with my interview because she invited me back a second time.

The second interview was three months later. She asked me about how I was still able to balance the various aspects of my life: family, career, community service, and the other activities that I was involved in. I shared my values and views of trying to help others and trying to show a work ethic that my family and colleagues would be proud of and perhaps copy. I was surprised that after the second interview to find out she nominated me for an *Entrepreneur of the Year* award for the year 2000 from a local organization that she belonged to. This was quite a pleasant surprise. Even though I did not win, it was still an honor to be mentioned among the elite, successful business owners in the community.

How Do You Do It All?

After my nomination, I decided to join the organization. During my first year, I managed to bring in the most advertising from local businesses. I was still working for the insurance company full-time, and concurrently with Mary Kay as a sales director, so people in the organization would ask me, as many others have and continue to do, "How do you do it all?"

I always offered that my energy stemmed from the help I was able to provide others and that helped me to be a "winner for the Lord" as the poem suggested.

In my first year with the organization, I was elected chairperson for the Aloha and Hospitality committees, co-chair for the Small Business Committee, co-chair for the Membership Committee, co-chair for the Installation Committee, co-chair for the Christmas party, a committee member for the Entrepreneur of the Year awards, and, if that were not enough, I was a committee member for the Annual Scholarship Golf Tournament! I had also recruited thirty-five new members from the community, most of them business owners. All this hard work produced positive results, and I was awarded a beautiful plaque for Most Outstanding Member of the Year.

In my second year with this organization, I was elected to the Board of Directors, co-chair for the Scholarship Gala, co-chair for the Annual Scholarship Golf Tournament, and co-chair for the Membership Committee.

In my third year, I was elected chairperson of the Membership Committee, chairperson of the Small Business Committee, co-chair of the Installation Committee, and co-chair of the Annual Scholarship Golf Tournament. I managed to bring in fifty new members into the organization and renewed many of the existing members.

A Winner for the Lord

I honestly felt that "I was a winner, not for me, but for the Lord." When I saw all the positive energy and outstanding results that we collectively earned, I knew in my heart I was making a difference in the personal and professional lives of many.

My success to that point with the organization encouraged me to consider running for the position of President Elect for 2002-2003. Despite my success and the appreciation given by many of the members, I discovered there was a small group of critics who took it on themselves to talk negatively to other members about me behind my back.

There was one member who said she would not vote for me because I had not been in the organization as long as she and she did not think I had people management skills or enough experience. I understood her doubts, but after considering all I had done for the group in the past three years, I did not believe they were valid reasons for me not to seek the position of President Elect. I felt

I had the most important skills, and those that I did not have, I would learn. I also believed the people I had recruited into the organization were supportive of me.

I did not win the election!

The election was a mail-in ballot. When I followed up with many of my friends, they said they had sent in their ballots. Yet the organization's secretary told me the ballots of over twenty of my friends had not been received. There was widespread speculation the election was not properly managed and monitored.

A few days after the election results were announced, a past President invited me to breakfast. She told me that she and her husband, who was also a former President, recognized the contributions I had made and all the time my efforts represented. She offered her hope that I would stay on with the organization and not quit. I responded that I am neither a sore loser nor a quitter and that I planned to remain and be as active as I was in the past. After all, how could I "be a winner for the Lord" if I quit?

Looking Back at the Face of Misfortune

I did just that. I remained involved in various committees and worked for the organization and its outreach programs. In 2003-2004, I was once again encouraged by members to run for President Elect. Another member had shown interest in running for the position and asked if she could run for President and me for Vice President. Since I was President for another nonprofit organization, the Hawaii Skin Cancer Coalition, I accepted her suggestion.

Other members of the organization called to encourage me to run for President, adding that they were confident that I could win. I responded that I had already given my word that I would seek the Vice President's position. Unfortunately, my decision was not well received by the other candidate for Vice President. He called me and asked me to run for the President-Elect position instead. He insisted that I should not run for the Vice President position.

He added that he already had many members that would vote per his suggestion. I was skeptical because he had made similar claims when I was running for President Elect the previous year. During that time he said that he had surveyed the members and advised me that about 75% of the members were going to vote for me. My intuition told me to simply take his input with a grain of salt.

Three days before the election, I called several members to ensure that they had indeed cast and mailed their ballots. One responded that he threw away the ballot because two Filipino men with heavy accents were calling him day and night to pressure him to vote for my opponent. I responded that I needed his help on this, and offered to fax him a fresh ballot that he could then fax to the organization's office. He agreed. The following day, the secretary gave me a call, telling me she had received his mail-in ballot and his fax, including his signature.

I called my friend back and asked, "So, you found your original ballot?" He said, "No, I threw that away. But, I did receive the ballot by fax, and I signed and returned that by fax."

He was curious about why I was asking. I explained that the office had received both his original ballot and the fax! He repeated that he had thrown away the original and had certainly not mailed it in. At that point, he and I were concerned that someone had forged his signature on the mailed ballot. He stated that he no longer wanted to be a part of this organization because of the "games" people were playing.

I learned later that day there were at least two other examples of suspicious activity, as the office had received multiple ballots from the same person. At that point, there was a growing concern among many of the members that something was definitely wrong.

The votes were counted and, once again, the decision was not in my favor. Despite the overwhelming expectation that I would win, I lost by many votes! My opponent celebrated his victory. I, and many of the people in the organization who believed in me, were deeply skeptical of the balloting process. Because of the suspicions, the Ballot Committee closely inspected the actual ballots received. It was discovered that many ballots were copies of the original ballots, not originals. The committee determined there were close to fifty fake ballots. An emergency board meeting was held.

Triumphant Truth

I was astounded that these people would go to the lengths they did to prohibit me from winning. This was a professional business organization and I did not understand how anyone would consider pulling these unethical stunts. I was hurt and disappointed, too, because of all the efforts and sacrifices I had made for the benefit of the organization and the community.

During the investigation, there was a great deal of *"He said, she said"* with people playing *the blame game*. To this day, nobody ever admitted to the suspected fraud. A second election was held, but this time by in-person voting. No more mail-in ballots! The results of this election were surprising. I won handily by a vote of 61 to 25. My opponent stopped celebrating.

Even though I won, the feeling remained that I was not entirely welcome in the organization by a select group. There was obviously a clique that had their own agenda and did not want me to succeed. I focused on the work that needed to be performed as this was a community organization and I was committed to make a difference in the community. Even with all that happened, I knew, as the poem suggested, *"People are watching and I am the example they will follow."* I set out to be a good example that others could be proud of and would perhaps copy in the future.

As the Vice President, I became involved as chairperson of the *Entrepreneur of the Year* event and continued to aggressively bring in new business members to the organization. Through the first half of the year, I worked hard and several of my friends in the organization began to bring up the issue of my running, once again, for the President position. These people believed not only in the things that I had already done, but in the energy and commitment my presidency would bring to the organization. They believed it could take the group to greater levels than it had experienced so far.

Fame Awaits Me: Beginning of Plan B

There were also some friends and members that discouraged me from running again. They asked why I would want to run again, considering all the grief of the past. Someone asked me why I did not put my efforts elsewhere; or, maybe start something new. Regardless of the discussions, I asked for their support given my commitment to the organization. Truthfully, I had already thought of an alternate plan if things did not work out here.

I had lunch with a gentleman who announced his plans to run for the President-Elect position. I offered the suggestion that perhaps he could run this time instead as Vice President, and I would run for President Elect, and then next term, I would support his candidacy for President. This idea came to mind because during the previous year's election, someone had asked me the same question. One reason that I wanted the Presidency that next term was there were many local businesses that not only expressed support for me, but who also pledged financial support to the organization once I was President. Unfortunately, my suggestion was rejected, but I had already made up my mind to go ahead with the election anyway, just one last time.

I started my campaign by working to get renewals of membership among my friends. Some discouraged me because of the prior elections; some did not want to renew and left the organization. I prayed to God to lead the way, to put me in the position where I could help the most, where I was needed the most. And, if it was not meant for me to win, then I will go ahead and follow my alternative Plan B.

I did not win!

I look back on this period, not with regrets, but with the acknowledgment that life lessons are sometimes painful to learn, but wisdom is a valuable commodity regardless of short-term disappointment. I recalled two of my favorite 'Paradoxical Commandments' written by Dr. Kent Keith:

"*If you do well, people will accuse you of selfish ulterior motives....* *Do well anyway.*"

"*The biggest men and women with the biggest ideas can be shot down by the smallest men and women with the smallest minds... Think big anyway.*"

I also recalled one of my favorite prayers:

Lord, I need to be a winner, not for me, but for you; People are watching and I am the example they will follow; Lord, I need to be a winner; to show someone else the way; I can touch more lives by being a success.

My friends told me that this small group of people had insecurity and jealousy issues and advised me to pay no attention to that attitude. I agreed. Their petty comments and actions could not compete with the many, many friends, business associates, clients, and family members who had supported me.

So, despite the small clique that was bound and determined to keep me out of the highest position, I came away from this experience all the better. I knew the confidence that springs from listening to and trusting the inner voice that compels me to do the right thing, regardless of the outcome. It helped me to further develop my *Million Dollar* Attitude. I also credit these experiences, while not pleasant, with my finding the vision and the will to go ahead with my Plan B.

LORD, I NEED TO BE A WINNER

Lord, I need to be a winner
Not for me, but for You
People are watching and I am
The example they will follow.

Lord, I need to be a winner
To show someone else the way;
I can touch more lives by being a success
So I need to succeed today.

Lord, I need to be a winner
And I'm willing to do my share
But knowing that all things good come from You
I need to know You're there.

Lord, I need to be a winner
Everyday You give me life
And with Your leadership and Your strength
I know I can succeed, in my business
And in my personal life.

And Lord, when You help me win
And I stand to tell my story
I'll always remember to give unto You
The praise, the Honor and the glory!

Author Unknown

The Paradoxical Commandments
by Dr. Kent M. Keith

www.paradoxicalcommandments.com

People are illogical,
unreasonable, and self-centered.
Love them anyway.

If you do good, people will accuse
you of selfish ulterior motives.
Do good anyway.

If you are successful, you will
win false friends and true enemies.
Succeed anyway.

The good you do today will be forgotten tomorrow.
Do good anyway.

Honesty and frankness make you vulnerable.
Be honest and frank anyway.

The biggest men and women with the biggest
ideas can be shot down by the smallest
men and women with the smallest minds.
Think big anyway.

People favor underdogs but follow only top dogs.
Fight for a few underdogs anyway.

What you spend years building may be destroyed overnight.
Build anyway.

People really need help but may
attack you if you do help them.
Help people anyway.

Give the world the best you have and
you'll get kicked in the teeth.
Give the world the best you have anyway.

CHAPTER 7
Beauty Pageants: From The Rice Fields To Las Vegas

Joni believes: "Dress for success; dress to impress."

"She is clothed with strength and dignity;
she can laugh at the days to come."
Proverbs 31:25 (NIV)

Dream Big – Even When "Petite"

When I was five years old, I dreamed of someday being in a beauty pageant. My "stage" then was the middle of a rice field, where the birds made a snack of the rice despite the not-so-effective scarecrow. I would stare at the sky and daydream, imagining that someday I would be a part of a real pageant. I had seen magazines where beautiful women were portrayed to be so glamorous. I realized that in the rice fields I was not so glamorous, but I could still dream.

Occasionally, my family would go to the cinema. Although I was not interested in the plot of the movie, I would admire how beautiful the women movie stars were. Living in a small Filipino province meant living surrounded by chickens, carabao, pigs, goats, rice fields, peanuts, and the ever-present dust from the unpaved roads. Add to this the lack of indoor water and plumbing, and no telephone or electricity, and I was a far cry from the glamorous women I saw in the movie house. Still, I kept my dream alive.

When I lived with my aunt, I would visit my older cousins next door and sneak into their shoe boxes and "borrow" their shoes. I pretended that I was one of the beautiful women in the movies. The thin heels of the shoes would penetrate the ground and made walking a challenge. Eventually, I had to put away the shoes. But, I never put away my dream. It stayed with me for many years, following me when I moved to Hawaii.

Mrs. Hawaii Filipina

In 2000, I was asked if I would be a contestant in the Mrs. Hawaii Filipina pageant that is held each year in Honolulu. Since there is a scholarship involved with this pageant, all contestants needed to raise money. The pageant contestants were judged in the areas of terno gown, which is the traditional Filipina formal attire, the talent competition, and an onstage interview. I had raised my self-confidence thanks to my involvement in Mary Kay, so I accepted the challenge.

There was much preparation involved, with general rehearsals, advertising, getting sponsors, selling tickets, and rehearsals for my own talent part, but I was willing to do all this to live the dream I had nurtured long ago as a little young woman in the Philippines.

One challenge came up: my General Agent at Guardian Life found out about the pageant and called me into his office. He said, "What are you doing? You only have 24 hours in a day; who do you think you are?" He threatened to fire me!

That didn't really faze me, because of my childhood dream. I had to keep going. I told him it was almost over and not to worry.

I was crowned as the First Runner-Up and overall the experience was tremendous. I enjoyed working with all the other women and getting to know them. At the same time, I shared with them about both Mary Kay and Guardian Life Insurance. Some of them became clients!

Again, Mary Kay Training Pays Off

In 2001, I was invited and encouraged to compete in another pageant, the Mrs. Honolulu International, which is more of an open competition for all ethnic groups. This time there was no need for fundraising. There were private interviews, an onstage interview, a gown competition, and a higher emphasis placed on the beauty and appearance of the contestants. The ability of the contestant to balance career, family, and community service efforts was also of high importance. This was yet another tremendous experience being with other women, getting to know them in a friendly competition and making new friends.

Being in the public eye because of my exposure with Mary Kay and Guardian Life Insurance, I was willing to work to improve my appearance. This included learning how to walk, talk, smile, make positive impressions, and carry myself. Once again, my Mary Kay background served me well in these endeavors. Going onstage and handling the private interviews was nerve-racking. I often asked myself why I put myself through these things. However, I knew that deep down these experiences would help me in many ways not yet known to me. I felt sure it would improve my effectiveness in approaching, and conversing with, business leaders, business owners, and entrepreneurs in the community. I was crowned as Mrs. Honolulu International, and this was a great feeling, especially because I was the only Filipina competing! Not only that, but the other contestants were quite a bit taller than me. Just taking part in a pageant, let alone winning the crown, was such a great experience. I thought back, once again, to my early days in the provinces and my dreams of somehow, someway, making this happen.

Fortunately, my General Agent didn't find out about this pageant until it was over and he saw my picture in my office.

He asked, "What is this?"

I said, "Gary, don't worry, it's over!"

Besides, I continued to keep my production high even while I competed in the pageant.

A few weeks later, I made an appearance at the State Capitol for a Child Abuse Prevention activity. I wore my Mrs. Honolulu International gown, sash, and crown. Little did I know that while I was being interviewed, it was being aired live on Channel 2. When I found out, I thought, "I hope Gary does not see this." But, as soon as I walked into the office, he said, "I saw you on T.V. this morning!"

I thought, "Oops! Here we go again."

In 2002, I was asked to compete for Mrs. Hawaii United States. I had a car magnet made saying "Mrs. Hawaii United States" and I was proud to put it on my car—except when I came to work at Guardian Life, I made sure to take it off so my General Agent wouldn't see it. One day, however, I was in a rush, and forgot to take it off. One of the other employees saw it and came in while I was talking to Gary and said, "Oh, Joni, I didn't know you were Mrs. Hawaii United States!"

I said, "How did you know?"

He said, "I saw the magnet on your car."

I looked at Gary and thought, "Oops, again."

Gary asked, "What is this now?"

I said, "Don't worry, it's over again."

To myself, I was also thinking, how am I going to tell him I have to go to the national competition in Las Vegas? There was no way I could tell the truth, because he would never allow me to go. So, I told Gary I was taking my family on vacation to Disneyland. He said okay to that.

As it turned out, another Guardian Life agent was booked on the same flight as I to Las Vegas! Oh, no! Word got out around the office and Gary called me at my hotel while I was rehearsing. We did not get to talk (whew!), but when I returned to the office, he said, in a loud voice, "Joni! Come to my office!"

I thought, "Uh-oh, here I go again." But, I was ready with my answer this time.

He said, "How come you did not tell me that you were going to Las Vegas to compete for Mrs. United States? I already know who won!"

I said, "Well, Gary, if I would have told you, I did not think you would allow me to go."

He said, "I'm going to fire you!" Then, he paused and added, "But, I can't."

I tried to explain, but he said, "You do not understand."

I cut him off and said, "No, Gary, you do not understand. This has been my lifelong dream. I am not getting any younger; I am getting older, and I felt this was my only chance to fulfill my dream."

I raised my right hand and promised him that this was the last pageant. I would never enter anymore pageants. But, a few months after this, I received a letter to compete for Mrs. World! It was very tempting, but I kept my word.

Despite these challenges, it was an honor to represent Hawaii in the national competition, competing with fifty-one beautiful, career-oriented women from around the United States and its territories. This was yet another dream come true.

I did have a twinge of insecurity (after all, I am human) as I was not only the shortest contestant, but the only Filipina as well. I was nervous about competing with so many tall, beautiful, mostly blue-eyed Caucasian, experienced women on a national platform. This insecurity subsided when I checked out the competition during the first day of orientation. I noticed three other contestants who could be described as "petite," or, in other words, short. This was a great relief, as I felt I had something in common with at least two others in the pageant! While this was helpful, I think being a part of Mary Kay taught me how to feel good about myself and how to feel tall no matter what my actual height, because I have so much to offer. However, I do admit, that seeing the three other 'short' contestants boosted my confidence!

My purpose in being part of this pageant was to be exposed to all these beautiful, intelligent, successful women, and to learn as much as I could about all facets of them as individuals. Being from Hawaii was a huge benefit. Everywhere the contestant group would go, people would notice the Hawaii sash and make comments like, "Oh, there is Mrs. Hawaii! We want to go to Hawaii someday. You are so lucky to live in Hawaii."

By just being from the State of Hawaii, I received a tremendous amount of attention, which was a huge plus for me. I enjoyed the special treatment. Everywhere we traveled, I routinely received compliments, free dinners, free cover charges at clubs, and strangers wanting a photograph with me. I felt like a celebrity!

There were many rehearsals and much planning for the big night of the pageant. This pageant, like the last one, included sessions to show us how to walk, how to present ourselves, how to talk, interview skills, and what formal gown to wear. It was a tremendous experience, and I gained much in both tangible and intangible ways. I kept thinking back to when I was a little young woman walking in the soft dirt in my cousin's high heels, trying not to sink in too much. Now, I was walking in my own high heels on a national stage in Las Vegas, Nevada!

Creating the Past One Day at a Time

I had tears in my eyes when I recalled my past and how my dreams had somehow come true. With God's guidance, my family's support, good fortune, and hard work, I was able to do the great things I had dreamed about so many years ago. Even though I was not crowned Mrs. United States, I considered this truly a wonderful experience. In the "Big Leagues" of pageants, I had held my own and met some wonderful women. A few months later, I heard, from Filipinas in the Hawaii community, gossip along the lines of "why would she continue to compete in these pageants… she is short!" I responded that *it is not so much about winning the crown, but rather the experience I had gained that enhanced my life in so many ways.*

I was and still am constantly striving to improve myself. The pageants were fantastic in bolstering my self-confidence for my career. Also, my involvement in the pageants has helped to serve as a role model to those who young women who have a dream, but, lack confidence - as I did when I was young. Much like Mary Kay, my personal hero, this was a way for me to help encourage women to develop their hopes and dreams, to become empowered in whatever they dream, and more importantly, to help them to believe in themselves.

CHAPTER 8
Honolulu Broadway Babies

Joni believes: "Life is daring or nothing."

"When I called, you answered me;
you made me bold and stouthearted."
Psalm 138:3 (NIV)

Meeting Kristian Lei

I was President of the Honolulu Skin Cancer Coalition in 2003-2004. I have been involved for many years in this coalition because I believe in spreading awareness about skin cancer. Living close to the equator as we do in Hawaii, the sun's power is dangerous if precautions are not taken by those who spend much time outdoors. We held a big annual event at the Ala Moana Shopping Center on what is known as "Center Stage." As part of the event, dermatologists were available to examine, free of charge, those who wanted medical advice. I enjoyed being part of this organization because when I lived in Arizona for two years, I had worked with six dermatologists. Every week, we would see dozens of patients who had precancerous skin conditions. We also witnessed some cases of melanoma, the most serious and deadly form of skin cancer.

During the 2004 event, I was in charge of the entertainment. While at a different function, I met Kristian Lei, who played the lead role of Kim in *Miss Saigon* in Europe. I had known of her for some time, but this was my first chance to meet this beautiful, talented young woman. I felt shy as I anticipated talking with her. Then, I went to the restroom and there she was!

Without hesitation, and because I was so excited, I screamed, "Kristian Lei! I have wanted to meet you for several years!" I don't think she was prepared for my enthusiasm in the bathroom. Later she confessed that she thought I was some "crazy woman."

I asked her if there was anyway she could sing for our Hawaii Skin Cancer Coalition event. I spoke with her husband, Gavin, who performed with her. I complimented their singing and mentioned my wish to have them sing at our event. We exchanged telephone numbers and they said I could call them about it. I think I left five messages for her, but never received a return call. Wondering why, I called Gavin to make sure she had received the messages. He agreed to talk to her about it. I was nervous since we were getting closer to the event. Luckily, Gavin called back and they generously agreed to perform for us.

With Kristian Lei's involvement, everything went well. Both she and the event were a success! Afterwards, Kristian mentioned her nonprofit project, the Honolulu Broadway Babies, which was preparing for its first event. She asked if I could help her to get sponsors. I invited her to visit my office and tell me more about the program.

Honolulu Broadway Babies

At our meeting, Kristian said she wanted to raise money for people with disabilities and those who are mentally challenged. She explained that her younger brother has Cerebral Palsy and she felt compelled to do all she could for him, as well as others similarly afflicted. One of her goals was to build a school for young people who needed more attention and development. She hoped this would help develop skill sets in these disadvantaged people, many of whom are intelligent despite their physical handicap.

I was moved emotionally when I heard her plans. My heart went out to her for doing such great things. Without hesitation, I agreed to support Kristian Lei's program, despite my crazy schedule, because I believed in her plans and her project. I asked her exactly what she wanted me to do. She asked me to seek financial support from businesses in the community.

Because I had a network of business relationships from Mary Kay, Guardian Life Insurance, colleagues and friends, I told her that I would do my best. Her Broadway Babies event was scheduled for the third week of August 2004. The event was a mixed plate of music and dance arrangements from various Broadway shows. She invited her friends who were professional singers and dancers, some of whom had performed around the world. In addition, she supplemented the professional "core" with local amateur and semi-professional talent.

Kristian was concerned with the tight schedule, the logistics, and the still unknown financial support from the community. Previously, she had asked some businesses and individuals for support, but much more was needed to pull off this big event. I focused on the task of getting the needed support. I went out into the community and was fortunate to be able to secure a higher level of financial support, including from my General Manager at Guardian Life Insurance Company of America. Whenever I received a payment, or pledge of support, I would call Kristian and she would be ecstatic to hear the good news.

I also encouraged many restaurants in the Honolulu community to support Kristian's Broadway Babies. When Kristian's nine professional performers arrived from the Mainland, the Zaffron Indian Restaurant, Dave and Busters, and Ruby Tuesday generously sponsored them and fed the entertainers for free. I also gained support from Ken Simon, President of Menehune Water, who donated many cases of bottled water for all the rehearsals and for the main event.

A Filipino-Russian Woman

One day, Kristian visited my office in mid-July, roughly one month before the show, and asked if I would be willing to perform in one of the numbers called "Cell Block Tango" from the movie and show *Chicago*. For those that have not seen the movie, the "Cell Block Tango" is about five women in prison who had all allegedly murdered their husbands for various sordid reasons. One of these women, a Russian woman in the movie, was not guilty and this is the woman that Kristian asked me to play. For this production, we would change her nationality from Russian to Filipina. I was so honored when she asked me to perform onstage with her and her friends from Broadway.

I was a natural in filling the role of a Filipina, but I told Kristian that I had never performed at that level of song, dance, or acting before. I told her I did not have the skills needed to perform in a Broadway-style musical.

She said, "Joni, I know you can do this! Seeing all of your awards, trophies, plaques, and all the other evidence of your accomplishments, I am convinced that you could rise to this challenge as well."

She encouraged me and offered to train me daily in vocals, dancing, and acting. Given this, I agreed to accept her gracious invitation, hoping it would be fun.

As I rehearsed with her, I was amazed at the intensity of the vocal training that included breathing exercises. She taped voice exercises so I could practice breathing and singing while driving. I am sure the people stuck with me in Honolulu traffic were concerned about this strange woman singing at the top of her lungs. For the dancing and acting, there was also much work to do to get me ready. And, my role involved me speaking lines, not just singing and dancing.

To give the local audience a laugh, Kristian not only "morphed" the Russian character into a Filipina, but also incorporated a Filipino slang term and nuance into the script. Those who have seen

Chicago may recall how the Russian's (now Filipina's) monologue ended with a heartfelt "NOT GUILTY!" In our version, we opted to speak the line "Not guilty!" with a Filipino accent that rose in pitch on the word "guilty!"

Everyone, including Kristian Lei, assumed that I could navigate this without any problem, but I had a hard time trying to make this sound as she wanted, with the local dialect. I practiced constantly, especially while driving down the highway with the window down. I repeated over and over, in a loud, expressive voice, "NOT GUILTY!" and tried to mimic the local accent. I remember a few motorists noticing this unusual behavior, likely thinking I was rehearsing for a court appearance. I wonder what their speculation was about my "crime," since I was driving a new Mercedes Benz and was well-dressed. White-collar crime, no doubt! With dedicated practice, I was finally able to sound like a Filipina in Hawaii, something Kristian originally believed I could do without training or practice.

How Did I Get to Be So Lucky?

The show was a great success. When the curtains first parted, I could not believe I was onstage next to those seasoned Broadway performers, and with all those people in the audience in front of me. What a feeling! I was excited and nervous at the same time. This was beyond my dreams, but Kristian believed in me and was determined that I could do it.

The most touching part of the show for me was the final song when all the cast came onstage. Kristian brought her brother, Joshua, to join in the singing. This reminded the audience the purpose of the show was to benefit the disadvantaged. We received a prolonged standing ovation, with thunderous applause, and I saw many people with tears streaming down their faces. I, too, felt emotional and teary, and I had a deep sense of satisfaction from being a part of Kristian's dream.

Through my involvement in the show, and the support I was able to enlist from the community, Kristian told me that I went far beyond her expectations. She confessed that early on she suspected that I may be one of those celebrity stalkers that you hear about. She hesitated to return my calls, but because of my persistence, she decided to take a chance and talk to me. She said she was glad that she did. In fact, she told me later that she had been praying for someone to help her with this big project. When I came along, it was a blessing to her.

I felt blessed too, because I have gained a lifelong friendship and Kristian is now like one of my baby sisters. I continue to support her career and promote her as a performer in special events.

What I was able to learn from this experience is that if I help others, then when I need help, others will help me. I asked Kristian to help me with my skin cancer event, and in turn she asked me for help with Broadway Babies. We were able to pool our different skills and networks, not only for us, but for the community. The sponsors who supported our events also helped the community and we hope the community will support them.

As I travel through life, I continue to recognize the value of relationships. After all, that is all we really have. So, I will continue to build good relationships that I can be proud to be a part of.

CHAPTER 9
FAMES: Filipino American Multi Ethnic Society

Joni believes: "We have a responsibility
to give back to the community."

"Serve wholeheartedly, as if you were serving
the Lord, not men, because you know that the Lord
will reward everyone for whatever good he does…"
Ephesians 6:7-8 (NIV)

Serving the Hawaii Business Community

I always believed God had a plan for me and that things happen
for a reason. Rather than feeling sorry for myself and lingering on
what happened with the experiences with the local organization, I
chose to believe God wanted to use me elsewhere to reach and help
more people. "Plan B" became my focus at the time. As I developed
my idea for a community-based nonprofit organization, I kept
thinking of my mentor, Mary Kay Ash. I imagined how she worked
through the challenges in her life displaying her famous *CAN DO*
attitude. I had my own attitude: a "Million Dollar Attitude."

Often, I woke in the middle of the night with my mind racing,
thinking about a new idea for a community-minded organization
that could benefit local small business owners and those considering
starting a business in Honolulu. This idea intrigued me as I tried to

develop an organizational mission, goals, and even a name. I tried to imagine how I would impact the community with a support organization that could make a difference beyond what was already available.

I met many people who said they did not know who to trust for their business start-up needs, such as insurance and other related employee benefits. I helped as many as I could, but I saw that these business people needed more widespread support. I formulated the idea of a new organization for the community that would provide mentoring, education, and networking. This is what I believed God wanted me to be involved in providing to the community.

I began to discuss and share my thoughts with local Filipino business leaders that I knew. I believed their input in the early formative stages would be helpful to solidify my thoughts and potential business plan. Several Filipino business leaders did not like the idea. An older Filipino business leader, whom I admired and whom I thought would encourage me to start a nonprofit organization, actually did not. In fact, he seemed insistent that I not follow through with my plan. He said there were already over 300 other Filipino-based community organizations. I understood his concern, but I believed I could offer an educational-based organization that could make a difference, regardless of how many other organizations were in the community. After all, I did not want to offer the same services the others were already providing. I had my own goals.

I found it interesting that when I spoke with local non-Filipino business leaders, they were more enthusiastic in their responses and offered their support. Many of those were business owners who had been in business for over ten years and who were successful, well-known in the community, and prosperous. They believed in my plan to help mentor and educate the local business community. Not only did they encourage me, they also pledged financial support.

FAMES Comes to Life

At the annual Filipino Fiesta at Kapiʻolani Park in Waikiki, I did the promotions and marketing for Kristian Lei and her nonprofit organization, Honolulu Broadway Babies, who performed on center stage. I was there to encourage Kristian as I believed in her, recognized her talent, and supported her goal of helping those in need in the Hawaii community.

After the performance, I was walking down the stairs fronting the stage, and a gentleman approached me, and said that he could help with Honolulu Broadway Babies. He introduced himself as Richard Cooks and said he had an extensive background in working with nonprofit organizations. I thanked him, adding that I was putting together a new nonprofit organization and I might need his help.

A few days later I met with him and spent a couple of hours explaining my thoughts, feelings, and purpose for this new adventure. He told me that he was married to a Filipina and that he understood what I was trying to do and believed in my idea. Richard immediately recommended that we get a Certified Public Accountant and begin work on obtaining 501(c)(3) nonprofit legal organization status. I was blessed to run into Richard Cooks. His enthusiastic support encouraged me even more. God was guiding me towards this dream by bringing people to me that could and would help.

I talked about Richard's advice with Jeannie Castillo-Barkley, a longtime Filipina friend who oversaw her own nonprofit organization, the Mother Earth Foundation. Jeannie introduced me to Allen Arakaki, a Certified Public Accountant, specializing in 501(c)(3) nonprofit organizations. The nonprofit organization status was important to me because this would enable me to get grants to support bigger projects for this new "Plan B" organization. Mr. Arakaki, along with attorney Brian Ezuka, helped tremendously in getting 501(c)(3) status for FAMES. Mr. Arakaki also gave me guidance on how to use my time wisely in starting a nonprofit community program.

I appreciated the time management tips, because this type of training had served me well with Mary Kay and with the insurance industry. For example, I developed a habit of always having a yellow pad and pen with me to write down ideas immediately as they occurred to me. I learned this technique from Mary Kay, who described in her autobiography how she would spontaneously "jot down" ideas when they would come to her. When I used my pad and pen, I felt like Mary Kay might have in her early days. I identified even more with Mary Kay when I learned she also encountered people who did not believe it would be possible to turn her ideas into reality.

As I saw my dream developing, I became excited. One of the first people I thought to call was my longtime friend and colleague, Yonie Malig-on. Yonie had shown tremendous support for me when I was with the other organization and campaigned for me relentlessly. She believed in my potential. She recognized the efforts and sacrifices I had made over the prior few years and was heartbroken when I did not win the prior elections. Yonie and I discussed my ideas and she offered sound and reliable feedback. Yonie recommended people who could help and might want to get involved.

I called a meeting at Remington College in downtown Honolulu. The college generously allowed us to use their facilities for our early meetings. I invited the most enthusiastic supporters and we brainstormed ideas to create a name for the organization. I wanted both "Filipino" and "American" to be in the title. After much discussion, we decided on "FAMES," which stands for "Filipino American Multi Ethnic Society."

Truthfully, not everyone liked the name FAMES, so I made extra efforts to get more feedback from business owners, managers and CEOs of large companies. I would ask them, "What do you think of the title 'FAMES' for the nonprofit organization?"

They were unanimously enthusiastic. They loved it! Not only that, they said they were proud of what I was doing to better the business community and offered to sponsor and support the new organization. Naturally, I left their offices on *Cloud Nine*, nearly bursting with joy.

I believe the name FAMES is an accurate description of the organization; and, it is a catchy acronym. The name represents a longer term goal of success, excellence, and fame.

Finalizing FAMES

From the beginning, I constantly thought about the variety of benefits that I could offer to FAMES members and the community.

I came across a flyer promoting a workshop provided by the Small Business Administration (SBA) and the Hawaii Women's Business Center (HWBC). I thought this would be a great workshop to attend to learn more. Even though I had a lot of experience, I believed, and still believe, there is always room for improvement.

At the end of the seminar, the audience was asked to give their reasons for attending. I responded that I was in the process of putting together a nonprofit organization for people starting small businesses or wishing to improve their existing business. The SBA and HWBC organizers expressed an interest in learning more. I invited them to a FAMES meeting. I offered them a table to display flyers, literature, and other promotional materials for their future workshops. They liked that idea because that would bring them more exposure and would promote their programs in a synergistic fashion, not in a competitive manner.

My experience with this seminar, and meeting the leaders of both the SBA and HWBC, reinforced my conviction to channel and connect people looking for assistance with their businesses. People who became frustrated when starting new businesses had often expressed to me a desire to quit. I believed that these people could use support, guidance, and mentoring to keep them going. I would tell them that "Quitters never win, and winners never quit, so keep going and have a can-do attitude!"

FAMES MISSION STATEMENT

After several meetings with my colleagues, the FAMES mission statement was created:

> The Filipino American Multi Ethnic Society (FAMES) is a local nonprofit organization created and designed to mentor, educate, motivate, and assist both existing and newly established businesses on how to become successful and profitable in their endeavor. It is also aimed to promote and develop strong leadership in the community.

FAMES First Fundraiser

With our mission defined, we began preparations for our first fundraising event. By that time, we had appointed officers and the board of directors, as this was needed for the 501(c)(3) application. For this first fundraiser, we started planning in mid-September 2005 with the target of late October. A Halloween costume contest with a live auction seemed to be a great plan. I had imagined this organization to be new, fun, and exciting, so I thought it would be a great idea to give away a Mercedes car. And, every woman attending would receive a beautiful long-stemmed orange rose, courtesy of Nancy Rosales, of Flower Impression, a good friend and client. I imagined these things, the Halloween costume contest, the live auction, and the new car give-away, long before planning the event. Mary Kay Ash had taught us to picture our goals and dreams. She would stress that "what you think about you bring about."

Despite the limited time to prepare for the fundraiser, I was determined to make it happen. The officers and board, with one exception, agreed that this could be put together in only one month. A meeting was held to give assignments to all, but one officer did not want to be involved as she seemed firm in her beliefs there was not enough time. During the meeting, I reassured everyone that 75% of what was needed for the event was already taken care of, so it should be "doable" to pull this event off. All I needed from everyone was to invite family, friends, and of course businesspeople.

Everyone was enthusiastic; however, the single dissenter still insisted that I get a second opinion from an event producer known within the Filipino community. To satisfy her, I tried to contact him, but I was not able to talk to him. She called the next day, curious if I had spoken to this person. I told her I left a message, but did not hear back and asked if it were so important that we contact him for a second opinion. She insisted that this be done and again voiced her concerns over the entertainment, video, photographer and who would feed them. I told her that all of the entertainers, video people, photographer, D.J., and others were long-time friends and clients of mine. They agreed to provide their services FOR FREE as they believed in our mission and wanted to help. I also told her not to worry about the smaller details of feeding these people as I had already lined up a restaurant that agreed to sponsor the meals for these volunteers.

I asked myself why I needed to get a second opinion given that most of the arrangements have been taken care of. What if this individual responded "Not enough time! Can't do it!" Does that mean that I should listen to that person? Why should I listen to this negative view when I knew we could pull it off? But, just to be sure, I sat down with our advisor and explained the entire situation, that 75% of the arrangements were in place, and he said, "It's doable."

A few days later, I got a call from legal counsel who said some of the officers and board members had called him complaining that "Joni is moving too fast."

I asked, "Who are all these people that are complaining?" I speculated that the complaints were likely from only one person. He grudgingly admitted that, yes, the complaints had come from only that one person. I told the legal counsel that the person in question was being negative about this and that I had everything in place. Rather than complaining, she ought to get with the program and start inviting people!

I also called our C.P.A. to get his opinion and suggestions on what we needed to do to make sure that all was well for us to go forward with the event. He said it would be acceptable to use another nonprofit organization's 501(c)(3) permit, and give them the customary 10% of the funds, since our application was in process with the state officials. So, I called around to the various nonprofit organizations that I was involved with and for whom I had volunteered. Some were willing to cooperate, but they wanted all the funds.

Jeannie Castillo-Barkley, a long-term friend and President and Founder of the Mother Earth Foundation, a 501(c)(3) nonprofit organization, agreed to help us, and agreed to the more manageable 10% of the funds going to her organization. She had appointed me as Vice President of the organization during that period. I was glad the Mother Earth Foundation would receive a percentage of the funds because it would help with planning their annual "Toys for Tots" program. The "Toys for Tots" program provides a special day for disadvantaged kids, with entertainment, food, gifts, and a Santa

Claus. This program resonated with me because as a child growing up in the Philippines, we could not afford to have Christmas gifts. Seeing the children's smiling faces when they received the gifts was rewarding for me.

The Need to Realign

Richard Cooks told me the dissenting officer called him, raising her voice, and even hung up the telephone on him. He called her back, mentioning that this was negative behavior, and that this was the first time that he had been treated this badly. He tried to be professional, but obviously she did not want to hear what she was being told. A few days later, that officer resigned as did another board member, who was her friend.

Despite these challenges and misfortunes, with a little over three weeks before the first fundraising event, rather than thinking about canceling the event, I was looking for a solution to make things happen. I asked a friend of mine, Rose Mendoza, if she might be willing to chair this event and be appointed as our FAMES Vice President. I explained to her our mission and the community benefits. She believed in the idea of FAMES and offered her support and accepted the Vice President position.

We worked closely together for the next three weeks. As time for the fundraiser drew near, everyone worked as a team. Things were shaping up nicely. I took it on myself to do as much promotion and marketing as possible. I took out advertising in the FilAm Courier, a local newspaper, and made interview appearances on Tiny Tadani's radio and television shows. Posters and flyers were placed in restaurants, offices, businesses, and in other visible areas to get the word out as much as possible.

No one gets a Free Mercedes Benz, until now

When I had imagined this fundraiser, I wanted it to be fun, new, and exciting, and felt that a Halloween theme would work out fine. Also, because of experience helping various pageants get new cars for the pageant winners, I had imagined having a new car giveaway to draw in a bigger crowd. For the FAMES event, I went right to the top, to the Mercedes Benz dealership in Honolulu, roughly four weeks before the Halloween fundraiser. My warm enthusiasm was met with the cool realities of the Mercedes dealer having a low budget for sponsorships for the remainder of the year.

Undeterred, I continued to ask for FAMES support from Mr. Lito Labuguen, an executive sales associate whom I knew, who then referred me to Mr. Dennis Rademacher, the General Sales Manager. Dennis and Lito both thought that my idea was an excellent one, but the final decision would be with the General Manager of the family-owned Mercedes dealership, Fletcher Jones III. My first conversations with Fletcher were not so promising. My request came at the tail end of the year and their marketing and sponsorship budget had been exhausted.

I persisted, and searched for "win-win" arguments to obtain Fletcher's support. I had already pictured the FAMES event, including the car, and this kept me going even though the first reaction to my request was negative. The second, third, and fourth reactions were similarly negative, but I was still determined.

Over and over I thought of how to frame my FAMES request in a way that would highlight the benefit to their company, in terms of goodwill to this new organization, which will help individuals starting a business to become successful. Once successful, these individuals would remember the kind gesture made by the Mercedes dealer, walk into the showroom, and buy their dream car. I think that framing the request in this way helped, because he finally asked if it were possible for FAMES and his dealership to share in the cost of the car. I then felt "Hurrah! There is hope!"

I met with the FAMES board of directors and officers to share the proposal from the Mercedes dealer. All agreed that this was a reasonable request and that we should go forward. Finally, FAMES and the Mercedes dealership came to an agreement and we were able to include the Mercedes Benz Giveaway on the posters, flyers, and media. This had a great impact on the turnout for the first fundraiser.

A funny thing: I heard many comments along the lines of "The Mercedes giveaway is just a gimmick; no way they could get a Mercedes for new organization!" I just kept quiet, ignoring the negative rumors, knowing that soon enough they would know the truth.

The 2005 Annual Fundraising Event

On the night of the fundraising event, we were pleased with the turnout. The crowd enjoyed the Halloween theme as it gave them the opportunity to get dressed up in an original way. Courtesy of Nancy Rosalles, each woman there received a beautiful long-stemmed orange rose. The Halloween backdrop turned out well, thanks to the work of Rose Mendoza and her husband Troy. The live auction, led by Joe Teipel, was a blast, and Justin Cruz, a local radio personality on 93.1 FM was the event's emcee.

Perhaps the most exciting part of the evening was the 2006 Mercedes Benz giveaway. We picked five names randomly from the audience, and each finalist was given a car key. Only one of the keys was the right one, and so the suspense built as each person stepped up to the car to see if his or her key would fit.

When the lucky recipient, Mr. Eugene Malalis, who was actually the last one to try, opened the new Mercedes, there was an explosion of applause from the audience. Mr. Malalis later became a sponsor and a member of the FAMES board of directors, not to mention an active supporter of the FAMES mission. We were fortunate enough to have the entire event videotaped by Marlowe Gungab, and overall the event was exciting and fun as well as successful in raising enough money to enable FAMES to begin planning its first "Strategies in Business" workshop.

FAMES Monthly Meetings

Keynote speakers are important to motivate and energize the group and I would actively search the community for suitable speakers. The primary criteria for the speakers are a "rags to riches" story. Someone who started with nothing, worked their way up, and despite the many challenges, made it. This is an important criterion as there have been many friends and clients that over the years have asked for guidance and advice on how to start a small business during times of setbacks or obstacles. In the business community, there are so many people that may have goals and dreams, but they don't surround themselves with the right people and tend to get discouraged, frustrated, and thus quit before they even get started. Given this background, the main purpose here is to provide these types of people with guidance and to put a real, live person in front of them to highlight the importance of accepting setbacks as part of the learning and growing process.

I also imagined having speakers from businesses that had challenges and trouble early on, and who overcame those obstacles and became successful. I believed that speakers having this type of background would help motivate our members and guests to work through their individual challenges and to keep going no matter what. I shared this idea with the officers and board of directors, who unanimously agreed with having speakers of this type at our monthly meetings.

Another idea that I shared with the board and officers was to have "Table Sponsors" for a small fee, during the monthly meetings. These individual businesses would set up a table with samples and brochures, and they could talk to the members and guests during the open networking time before the start of the program. These Table Sponsors would also get to give a three-minute presentation during the program to promote their business.

FAMES got into pretty good shape right off the bat. The monthly meetings have been well attended, and potential spots for Table Sponsors have been sold out for months in advance, with a waiting list now in place for future meetings. At each meeting there is time set aside for open networking and talking with the various table sponsors. A typical FAMES meeting is organized in roughly the following fashion:

6:30 – 7:00 pm	Networking; visiting table sponsors
7:00 – 7:30 pm	Welcome by President and Founder
	Invocation
	Recognition of that month's birthday celebrants
	Dinner
7:30 – 8:00 pm	Introduction of Guest Speaker
8:00 – 8:30 pm	Introduction of Table Sponsors
8:30 – 8:40 pm	Recognition of New Members
8:40 – 8:50 pm	Introduction of all attendees
(name and business)	
8:50 – 9:00 pm	Announcements, Door Prizes, Closing Remarks

Free Full Day Workshop Offered

Because of the success of the fundraisers, FAMES was able to hold its first annual workshop entitled "Strategies for Business Success" in August 2006. It was a free, all-day workshop that included breakfast and lunch. Its purpose was to fulfill the FAMES mission to provide support, mentoring, and education for those wishing to start their own small business or for those wanting to improve an existing business.

Sonia Aranza, a long-time friend of our Vice President, Rose Mendoza, agreed to be our featured guest speaker for the workshop. Sonia is a Management Trainer and Consultant specializing in diversity and cross-cultural communications. She has an impressive resume notable for her many Fortune 100 clients, including IBM, Johnson & Johnson, Texaco, NASA and US Postal Service. Sonia has received such honors as the Asian-American Woman of the Year in 2002 from the National Association of Professional Asian-American Women. Sonia's presentation was, by all accounts, motivational and sincere.

Dr. Richard Schuttler, an international keynote motivational speaker, author, and management consultant also spoke on the subject of raising an existing business to a higher level of efficiency and production. Dr. Schuttler's presentation was informative and practical for all business owners and operators. We were fortunate to have these two professionals as part of our first workshop. Also, FAMES invited four other speakers, who discussed small business start-up, business plans, choosing the right business structure, business financing, sources of business loans, financial planning fundamentals, and an introduction to eBay.

As the time drew near to begin the workshop, it became clear the marketing and promotional efforts done earlier had been worth it as the room quickly filled to capacity. All the speakers were prepared and offered useful insights on various topics that entrepreneurs and small business owners found useful. The feedback, during and after the event, was along the lines of "Wow, this is an awesome production!" This was confirmed by the evaluation forms that which had many comments of "outstanding," "inspiring," "exceeded expectations," and "wonderful food." The workshop was videotaped and selected parts are on the FAMES website at www.fameshawaii. org.

The first workshop was successful beyond our expectations and the FAMES officers and board of directors began immediately to plan for our second FAMES workshop for 2007. They decided that the second fundraiser should follow a similar path as the first, with the Halloween theme, live auction, and another Mercedes to giveaway.

Planning for the 2007 Annual Workshop

Everything was going well for the 2006 fundraising event to generate funds for the second FAMES full day workshop in 2007, until I walked into the Mercedes dealership. Frankly, I expected my request to be met with an "Of course we'll give you another new Mercedes!" I mean, after all, I came in earlier in the year this time. That is what I was expecting. Unfortunately, I felt a sense of déjà vu all over again, as Fletcher Jones III said that he would talk to Dennis, who was not too certain that they could provide another new Mercedes this time as it was not in the budget.

Dennis seemed to be a supporter of FAMES, so I continued to make regular visits to the showroom to help win them over again. One time I was talking with Dennis, when Fletcher happened to walk by. I mentioned, "Oh, Fletcher, we were just talking about you!" and proceeded to go over the salient points of the reasons this would benefit them.

When Fletcher said, "All right, we'll do it," I jumped out of my chair and gave him a hug. Immediately after that, I produced the written agreement, which I had in my folder, and had him sign it before he had a chance to change his mind. What a victory!

Needless to say, the second fundraiser for the 2007 workshop went exceedingly well. I appreciate Jojo Serina, along with his friend Glenn Sagayadoro, for contributing their talents to design the program. It was fabulous! Also, I want to thank John Noland from Radio K-108 for doing a spectacular job as our emcee and for continuing to promote our FAMES events. As this book is being written, we are planning our second FAMES workshop.

Powerful FAMES Team

I want to sincerely thank the following officers and directors for their support and belief in the FAMES purpose and mission:

Vice President, Rose V. Mendoza; Secretary, Sue Ann Lu, Assistant Secretary, Sara Jane A. Castro; Treasurer, Paul Lemcke; Assistant Treasurer, Gloria Poland; Auditor, Yonie Malig-on; Advisor, Richard Cooks; Legal Counsel, Bryan Andaya, J.D.; and the Board of Directors: Espie Badua, Mary Jean Castillo-Barkley, Vince Cervantes, Cherryl Cunanan, Charles Degala, Marites Keliikoa, Nilda Quindara, Eugene Malallis, and Willie Saturnino.

Mahalo to our Generous Sponsors

Mercedes-Benz

 DR. LAWRENCE TSEU, DDS

 Sue Ann Lu Agent — FOOD QUALITY LABS — ROYAL PALM GROUP

123 College

  *hello*World HAGADONE

Butler Enterprises Hawaii, LLC  **NORDIC** CONSTRUCTION, LTD. Menehune Water Company

 *Curves*  .G.S. CONCEPTS & PRODUCTIONS www.jagsproductions.com

 SendOutCards — Sound Mixer Production — HWBC

JT Production

Flower Impressions

NIGHTINGALE MANAGEMENT, INC.

ЧM Productions — *Raymond Young Photography*

 PLANET PHiLiPPiNES

CHAPTER 10
BNI: Business Network International

Joni believes: "Winners never quit, quitters never win."

"Let us not become weary in doing good,
for at the proper time we will
reap a harvest if we do not give up."
Galatians 6:9 (NIV)

What Is BNI?

In 2006, Cherryl Cunanan, one of the directors of FAMES (Filipino American Multi Ethnic Society) invited me to attend a BNI (Business Network International) meeting. Six years earlier, I had been approached about BNI and was told that it was a networking group that allows for only one person from each profession to join and that members work to refer business to one another. Truthfully, I was not impressed with that first meeting because there were only four people present and all we did was talk and have breakfast at a local golf course. At the time, I did not see the value in becoming a member.

When Cherryl invited me to her BNI meeting, I recalled my first impressions and politely declined. She was insistent, suggesting that her group was different from what I had experienced several years earlier. As a favor to Cherryl, given all her support of FAMES, I attended. I was pleasantly surprised to find over thirty business professionals at the meeting. There was a positive, energetic attitude among attendees. They followed a clear agenda and were more professional and businesslike than I expected.

When Cherryl asked me to go with her to BNI the following week, I wanted to attend. I did not join right away because I was concerned the time constraints of my busy schedule would make it difficult for me to attend the weekly meetings. However, a few BNI members asked me to substitute for them when they could not attend their meetings. Before I knew it, I was attending BNI meetings week after week. I enjoyed meeting with these people. I looked forward to going and I invited other friends to attend, even though I was not a member yet!

Attitude Change

I realized that my attitude towards BNI was changing. I viewed the weekly meetings more as a positive and educational experience rather than a chore that might interfere with my busy schedule. I found that once I changed my thinking and viewed the time per week as continuing education, that I was excited to attend the meetings. I realized the value of networking and meeting many new colleagues and friends, and it eventually resulted in new business for me.

During the time I was attending the BNI meetings, I was organizing the first FAMES fundraising event. I made sure to invite the entire Honolulu Metro BNI Chapter. Some of their members turned into close friends. One in particular, Sue Ann Lu, also became a FAMES Gold Sponsor.

I offered the BNI members a free table to display their products and company information if in return they would provide items to be auctioned off at the fundraiser. Kathy Davenport, the president of the Honolulu Metro BNI Chapter, agreed. My goal was to have

Kathy recognize the FAMES organization and become an advocate for it as I had for BNI.

BNI Chapter President

I sensed that Kathy was impressed by how I orchestrated a successful event in such a short time, with the help of the FAMES officers and board of directors. A few days after the FAMES event, Kathy called and said she wanted me to be the incoming president of a new BNI chapter. I told her I understood her confidence in me and that I would consider her kind offer. I needed to evaluate it after considering everything else I was committed to and responsible for in my life. I was focused on my career with Guardian Life Insurance Company of America, where I had committed myself to being number one nationwide in production. I also had to concentrate on preserving my position as team leader for Mary Kay cosmetics. In addition, I was still setting up the FAMES organization and volunteering in various community organizations.

The most important part of my life, my family, needed me, too. My nephew at the time was fighting for his life because of malignant brain cancer that needed surgery, chemotherapy, and other complicated medical treatment. It took much of my time and emotional energy to help him and our family. I had to do this for my sister, who had always been supportive of me. I did not see how I could fit in one more activity.

Kathy called again wanting to know if I had considered her offer. I responded that I did not feel comfortable accepting the opportunity then because of the competing priorities in my life. She would not take no for an answer, saying, "Oh no, don't back out on me now!" I told Kathy I would reconsider and give it further thought. It occurred to me that BNI and FAMES could complement each other in a synergistic way. In addition, in BNI I would represent Guardian Life Insurance Company of America and every week I could educate BNI members about personal and business insurance needs. I mulled over these advantages, and then Kathy and I talked again. I agreed to preside over a new BNI chapter. In the back of my mind, I was thinking, "Am I nuts? What am I doing now?"

I went to Kathy's next BNI chapter meeting where she announced forming five new BNI chapters. Kathy was looking for people who could join them. We were all given training on how to invite guests and how to properly conduct BNI meetings, which all have the same agenda and are conducted in the same manner. Kathy had assigned people to the various chapters and I learned she had assigned Eddie Goldman and Linda Nakanelua to other start up chapters. Eddie, a Realtor, was a client and friend of mine for over seven years and he insisted on being in my chapter. Since Eddie and Linda were friends, Linda also wanted to be in my chapter. Our small three-member group began thinking about other potential members and the various professions we wanted in our chapter. We started inviting three or four guests every week to build up the membership.

Making of the *Million Dollar Chapter*

We met every Thursday and soon people noticed that our chapter was growing faster than the other four start-up chapters. After we had ten members, Kathy told us that if we increased membership to fifteen, we could become our own 'stand alone' chapter. When that happened, I would officially be appointed as President, with Danny Bohlman, a photographer, who Eddie recruited, as Vice President, and Eddie as Secretary/Treasurer. We were excited and inspired to grow our membership to fifteen, so we could become our own chapter.

Kathy asked us to pick a name for our chapter. We had a brainstorming session and I asked everyone to offer their suggestions for a chapter name. I suggested the "Million Dollar Chapter" adding that this represented a striving for excellence, and made you 'dream big' and set higher goals. All agreed and we were now the "Million Dollar Chapter" of BNI Hawaii. We went forth in search of five more members.

We were stuck at fourteen members for a few weeks. Then, Dayna Hillcrest, who owned a small business with her husband, said that she wanted to join but that she had other commitments and might come onboard next month. I was determined to get to independent chapter status as quickly as possible, so I spoke with Kathy and asked if there was a way to have the prospective fifteenth member provisionally join so we could go forward with the chapter's independent status. Kathy spoke with Joann Seery, the Executive Director of BNI Hawaii, and together they approved our chapter for independent status. We got excited about this, calling Dayna our "Lucky 15."

The Million Dollar Chapter Finds a Home

Next, we needed to find a location to hold our weekly meetings. I suggested Dave and Buster's Restaurant at Ward Centre since we held the FAMES meetings there. That location worked well for FAMES, especially since there was plenty of free parking, something that is not common in Honolulu. Kathy, who had since been promoted within BNI to Area Director, was not impressed with this setting. She noted the noise from the games outside and she thought the lighting in The Showroom, our meeting area, was too dark. However, Danny, Eddie, and I agreed the showroom was set up nicely as a meeting room. It had a podium, microphone, and large screen to enable presentations. And, it was large enough to enable us to grow. In the face of such solidarity, Kathy approved Dave and Buster's as the meeting place for the *Million Dollar Chapter*.

We had only six weeks to prepare for the official BNI "Kick Off Day" for the Million Dollar Chapter. The date was set for June 8, 2006. We asked every member of the chapter to send out fifty invitations to business owners, as well as their business associates and friends. Kathy told us the largest chapter in BNI's history had thirty-seven members at its first meeting "Kick Off." She said if we had thirty-eight members, or forty to be on the safe side, then the **Million Dollar Chapter** would be Number One in first meeting membership.

It Has Never Been Done – Until Now!

I responded, "Why stop at forty? Let's go to fifty!"

Kathy said that forty would be the largest chapter to begin its first official meeting. But, I was determined that the Million Dollar Chapter was going to be even bigger!

Danny, the Vice President, when he heard my goal of being Number One with fifty members asked me if I were crazy. After all, then, we had only nineteen members.

I then challenged myself and my team to make BNI a top priority during the short time we had left before the Kick Off date. I sensed that my team and I would respond well with a challenge. Often, to achieve greatness, one must extend oneself and work to be better than they would have been otherwise.

Hard Work Pays Off

Whether I was walking, talking, driving, or sleeping, I put my mind to work on how to get the "right people" into our BNI chapter. The "right people" I looked for were business owners, top management, and leaders within the community. If BNI could benefit their businesses and careers, then I had to find a way to talk to them. I had to get creative!

When driving, I would look for vans and trucks with business logos, telephone numbers, and other contact information. At the time, I was personally looking for a rain gutter company for my home and had postponed the repair since I didn't know anyone in that business. One day I saw a van with "Rain Gutters" printed along the side, so I picked up my pen and jotted down the company name and telephone number. I called the owner. First, I told her that I needed her service, and then I asked if she had heard of BNI.

She had not and I explained a bit about BNI and invited her to be my special guest. She attended a meeting and saw all the members doing their required "60-second commercial" about their businesses in front of the attendees. This was a problem for her, because she said she was terrified to talk in front of people. I asked her to give me her overall opinion of the meeting and the people. She was positive in her remarks, except for the "speaking in front of the group" part. She said she would think about this and that I could follow up with her later.

Undeterred, I started asking my friends if they needed rain gutters and I found two people who needed her services. I called, enthusiastically offering three clients for her: myself and my two friends. I again expressed my wish to have her be a part of my BNI chapter. She agreed, and I met with her and gave her an application to fill out. She realized the potential of the being part of the networking group.

Then, I told myself that we needed a florist on the roster, so I reached out to a friend and another acquaintance who each owned flower shops. They both showed some interest, but not enough to attend the meetings. Determined not to give up, I literally went door-to-door in search of a flower shop that might want to join. I walked into Aloha Island Lei and Floral on Cooke Street in Kakaako and talked with the owner, Dave.

I asked him, "Would you like to grow your business and have more customers?" He replied, "Yes, of course I would."

He had never heard of BNI before and so I explained the goals of BNI and the "Givers Gain" philosophy that is BNI's trademark. I highlighted the importance of building relationships and having a BNI sales force working on his behalf. He was curious about my background, which I explained briefly to him. He had heard of Mary Kay, adding that if I were to pick him up in a Mary Kay "Pink Car," then he would agree to take a look at BNI and attend a meeting. I agreed to pick him up at 9:00 a.m. the following day,

Thursday, and bring him to the BNI meeting. I told him that I had traded my pink car for a black car because my kids did not enjoy being picked up from school in a pink car. He laughed.

I showed up at 9:00 a.m. sharp the following morning. "Are you ready?" I asked. He responded, "Oh, you are here!" He was surprised that I really was there to pick him up!

I asked him to bring along some brochures and business cards so the BNI people would understand what he does and what services his business provided. Still bewildered, he gathered them and we went to the meeting.

I went back to his shop later that afternoon. I did not have the chance to talk with him after the meeting because his son picked him up. I wanted to get his opinion of the BNI meeting. He said that he liked the group, but he thought he might be too busy to attend the meetings. I followed up again one week later, trying to convince him to join BNI. I expressed our wish to have fifty members and my belief that one of these members should be a florist. As an added incentive, I promised that if we reached fifty members, I would order fifty leis and balloons from his flower shop for our Million Dollar Chapter "Kick Off" day. He agreed, saying that he would do it mostly for me, to help me out with the BNI chapter.

Door-to-Door

Another example of my door-to-door efforts in recruiting new BNI members was the Platinum Detailing business. Whenever I drove on King Street, I would notice this auto detailing business, which always appeared busy. I made it a point to drop in and check them out to see if they could detail my black car. Of course my other purpose was to tell them about BNI and to get them onboard as a new Million Dollar Chapter member.

I drove in and asked an employee if I could speak with the manager or owner. He pointed out Alex, and I shouted, "Hi, Alex. How are you today? Are you Filipino?" He looked Filipino to me, but it was hard to tell since he was wearing sunglasses. He looked at me as if to say, "Do I know this woman?"

He responded, "No, I am Chinese!"

I told him that I was Chinese, too. What a coincidence! I jokingly added that his employees all seemed to be Filipinos. He answered that they are all Laotians! I responded, "Oops. They look Filipino to me."

Thankfully, he found this exchange humorous and we both started to laugh. I told Alex that I would like to have my car detailed and we went into his office. I was thinking, "This is my chance to talk with him about BNI."

He had not heard of BNI and I gave him my best pitch for how it could benefit his business. I gave him brochures and flyers with more BNI information. I added that we wanted to have fifty members for our Kick Off that was only a few days away. He wanted to talk it over with his girlfriend and asked me to call him the next day. Following the BNI discussion, he quoted me $104 for the detailing service. I just about fainted, thinking that I usually get my car washed at McKinley Car Wash for $12! Arghh, the things I do for BNI! I should note the detailing was worth it, with my black car glistening like new.

Rather than call Alex as he was expecting, I decided to drop by his shop and pick up his completed application. I asked if he had discussed this with his girlfriend, and he unfortunately had not. Given the looming deadline for the Kick Off day, I thought, "How can I convince him now, since I need his application today?"

We went back to his office and I once again tried to show him how this BNI chapter could benefit his business. Naturally, I had the application ready for him to fill out. He decided to join and started filling out the application. I was so thankful that he had agreed, especially since he had never attended a BNI meeting and had only my word to go on. With the application filled out and with a check in hand, I left, reminding Alex to show up on our Kick Off day.

Not Giving Up

In the final days before the Million *Dollar Chapter* Kick Off, I was busy meeting people and picking up applications. Kathy Davenport noticed this and asked how she could help. I gave her names and telephone numbers and asked if she could arrange to pick up the applications for me. Kathy obliged and laughingly described her efforts as "meeting strangers on the street, getting their completed applications, giving them a quick hug, then on to the next one." Anyone following her would have wondered what the heck she was up to. We shared a good laugh about this.

On June 7, we had our monthly FAMES meeting. I had to prepare for that, but at the same time I was dealing with recruiting as many new BNI chapter members as possible before the Kick Off date, which was the following morning! I had already managed to get forty-seven members lined up and was short only three new members.

I asked myself, "How can I find three more at this late date?"

Even though we had already broken the BNI record, I was determined not to quit. Besides, I had already ordered fifty leis and balloons for the fifty new BNI Million Dollar Chapter members. We had to have fifty.

I looked around the room just before the FAMES meeting at the variety of people present. At this point, Dr. Richard Schuttler walked in. I had not met him before, but I thought he would be a good candidate for BNI because of his profession as an international motivational business speaker. And as luck would have it, he was the scheduled guest speaker for the FAMES meeting that night. As he was getting ready to sit down, I went up to him and asked if he would join BNI and if he had received the BNI invitation that I had already sent to him. He responded that he had, and I asked him directly if he would join as a member of my BNI Million Dollar Chapter, thinking that he would be Number 48.

He asked, "Do you want me to?" I naturally said, "Of course I want you to!" Without the slightest hesitation, I asked him, "Before you speak, could you fill out the application and provide a check?"

He agreed! I ran to the women's room and called Kathy with the good news that we now had forty-eight members. She was laughing as I told her that Dr. Schuttler was filling out the application as we spoke.

At that point, I was actively, if not desperately, searching the room for Number 49. I went back into the FAMES room, thinking, "Who else could benefit from BNI?"

I saw a woman who I considered a good candidate and I asked if she could join that evening. She mentioned that she had been a member of BNI at one time and was familiar with the organization. She mentioned that if she were to join BNI again, she wanted to be with our chapter because of our energy and spirit. She wanted to think about it, but I convinced her there was no need to think! She could be inducted tomorrow at our Kick Off meeting. She agreed and I gave her the application. Once again I grabbed my trusty cell phone, ran to the women's room, and called Kathy with the good news that we had Number 49 onboard. Once again, she laughed and was excited by the news.

Then, it was down to the elusive, magic Number 50.

I returned to the FAMES meeting, scanning the room for candidates, with only a couple of minutes before the meeting started. I kept telling myself I had to get fifty members to turn my vision into a reality. Then, it hit me! My husband and I had started my limousine business just months before. It would be great to have the limo business represented in the BNI chapter. It was such an obvious choice that I wondered why I had not thought of it before. I discussed this with my husband Tom and asked if he would like to represent the limousine company. He agreed on the spot, without hesitation. He did not have any other choice!

"What a wonderful husband I have!" I told him.

It was great! One last time, I ran to the women's room and called Kathy with the great news. This was a dream come true! Kathy was ecstatic and congratulatory.

50 BNI Members

I was "at peace with the world" as we started the FAMES meeting. It was such a relief to know that we made it to fifty members. I thanked God for giving me the courage and determination to make my goal, and remembered the saying "Winners never quit and quitters never win."

The FAMES meeting went well that night and I was looking forward to the next day and our BNI Kick-Off meeting. Some of my friends teased me about it. Since the FAMES meeting ended at 9:00 p.m. and we would be back at Dave and Buster's early the next morning for the BNI meeting, which was scheduled to begin at 9:30 a.m., some suggested that I just bring a sleeping bag and pillow and camp out at Dave and Buster's.

I went to bed excited, thinking of how the room would be filled with fifty new BNI Million Dollar Chapter members. I imagined balloons everywhere and the beautiful leis for the new members. The next morning, we arrived at Dave and Buster's early to get ready for the joyous event. Some of the BNI members, including Danny and Eddie, were helping to ensure a great start.

I had promised Alex from the auto detailing shop that I would introduce him to the BNI members and told him not to worry about being shy or speaking in front of a group of people. I was pleased when I overheard Alex telling other BNI members, "I want to be just like Joni. She is such an excellent salesperson and had me filling out the BNI application forms without fully understanding what BNI is all about." The members were laughing at his remarks and, more importantly, were setting up appointments with Alex to have their cars detailed.

The first day of the BNI Million Dollar Chapter went well. I received positive comments from everyone. Kathy was impressed with the new chapter being the record-breaking, fastest-growing chapter in the State of Hawaii since BNI started in the 1980s. Both Kathy and Joann Seery, the Executive Director for BNI Hawaii, felt that our *Million Dollar Chapter* could be among the top five international chapters. This was amazing considering that BNI has organized almost 5,000 chapters in thirty-five countries. We were so excited that our new chapter ranked in the top five internationally and, of course, for being Number One in the State of Hawaii.

BNI Showcase

Throughout its first year, the Million Dollar Chapter was a "showcase" chapter for BNI. Other BNI chapters routinely sent their members to our meetings to encourage them to improve their own chapters and to take notes on how our chapter runs. At each BNI meeting we report the dollar amount of the business that has been passed from the group's referrals. This provides our guests and visitors with justification about why the BNI chapter could benefit their business and be worthy of their participation. They tend to be impressed with our *Million Dollar Chapter's* energy, enthusiasm, and the great results the BNI sales team brings to all.

I believe the best way to build a business is through personal relationships. I encourage everyone to adopt the "Givers Gain" philosophy of the BNI organization. "What goes around comes around" is a saying that aptly describes the BNI mind-set. If you give a referral to someone in the chapter, even though that specific person may not reciprocate, others will. It is a powerful and positive philosophy that helps bring the group together and helps all our businesses grow and prosper.

When I am at community, social, and professional events, I find that as I talk with strangers to learn of what they do, the thought always occurs to me, "How can my chapter members be of support to this person, and how can this person help my chapter members?" In other words, I find that I am constantly looking out for the *Million Dollar Chapter* and those first fifty members who helped make my dream come true.

I enjoyed a great journey during that first year as the President of the Million Dollar Chapter. It means a great deal to me to have grown this chapter from its start to its status today as the Number One chapter for the State of Hawaii. Of course, I could not have done this alone, and I offer a debt of gratitude to the Vice President, Danny Bohlman, whose organization and detail-oriented skills were a perfect fit for the organization. Also, I'm grateful to the chapter Secretary and Treasurer, Eddie Goldman, who did an exceptional job. The three of us put our individual, unique talents together and were able to push our chapter to the top. In any organization, if you are able to communicate well and work towards a common goal, you become more productive and positive.

I will always cherish and remember this part of my life. Since it is BNI's policy to have a new President instated every year to give other members a chance to develop their management skills, I have stepped down after finishing my term. I remain as an enthusiastic and active member and I am excited to serve as a Visitor Host. I wish the incoming President, and all future Presidents, the same good fortune and fellowship that I experienced in the first year.

DON'T START THE DAY
WITH DOUBTS AND FEARS

Don't start the day with doubts and fears;
For where they live, faith disappears;
Love won't grow in a gloomy heart
Where sorrows live and teardrops start.

Don't give up before you've begun
You still have time to get things done;
Don't waste the time God's given you;
Let Him be praised in all you do.

Don't be a quitter-You're not alone
We all must crawl before we're grown;
There are no rainbows without rain
There are no victories without pain.

Don't let God down and run away:
You can't go back to yesterday....
Don't start the day with doubts and fears;
For where God lives, Faith reappears!

Author Unknown

CHAPTER 11
Coincidence Or Destiny?

Joni believes: "Things happen for a reason."

**"For I know the plans I have for you,"
declares the LORD, "plans to prosper
you and not to harm you, plans
to give you hope and a future."
Jeremiah 29:11**

My Perfect Husband

They say, in regards to marriage, that the second time around is better. Even though I was not really looking, my husband appeared right before my eyes.

Tom and I met in the "Love Elevator." I was in an elevator with three of my friends, all Filipina, enroute to a Mary Kay glamour makeover workshop. As we went down on the elevator, it stopped on the 12th floor. This good-looking *haole* (Caucasian) man came in. The four of us were chit-chatting in Tagalog, the official Filipino dialect, and I noticed the gentleman listening intently. Before we reached the ground floor, he spoke to us in Tagalog. He had a pretty good accent actually!

He said, "Good afternoon, ladies. I also speak Tagalog."

The response was swift. We all burst into laughter as it is indeed rare to have a Caucasian man behave in such a manner. We exchanged contact information and I invited him to a Filipino-style get-together later in the week. I learned that he not only eats Filipino food, he likes it! The chemistry between us was apparent pretty much from when we met. People that know us now say things like "You guys are ALWAYS laughing and happy all the time." Thus, the place where this began is now affectionately termed "The Love Elevator." The rest is history.

My husband, Tom Yundt, is a Senior Aviation Engineer and he travels the Pacific Basin and Southeast Asia tending to airports in such places as Kosrae, Pohnpei, Yap, Mindanao, Palau, Saipan, and West Tinian. Our friends joke that no one is really sure where those places are. Many of his friends and colleagues suggest that he is somehow involved in covert operations for the government. But, he assures me that he is not; he's just doing "airport stuff."

One of my husband's favorite sayings is, "Behind every woman CEO is a surfer." He is very supportive of me, thinks my *Million Dollar Attitude* is wonderful, and that it complements his "Million Peso Attitude" really well. Tom told me he will be surfing 'til he is 100 years old. I said I will be wearing high heels 'til I'm 100!

We balance each other, and have always found it easy to compromise, and have not had issues about arguing or fighting. With trust, love, understanding, give-and-take, and a sense of humor, there is no reason to quarrel.

We were at a dinner recently with some of his boyhood friends, and one of the more intuitive exclaimed, "You guys are opposites!" True. But, hey, opposites attract. We always have a wonderful time together.

I thank God for blessing me with Tom.

From Jeepney to Limousines

In 2006, I started a new business in Honolulu, a limousine service. People have asked me why I have decided to start this business. It began with an early fascination with limousines. Over seven years ago, I even bought a small, white model limo and displayed it in my office. I looked at it from time to time and visualized myself in it. The few times I have been treated to a limo ride, it made me feel very special.

When my parents celebrated their 50th wedding anniversary, I wanted to surprise them by picking them up in a limousine, taking us all to church, then on to a restaurant. I found out pretty quickly that there were no limousines available that day from the many limousine companies in Honolulu. I had to really beg to get someone lined up! That day turned out well, and Mom and Dad were thrilled with the limo ride.

After this anniversary, I was asked to assist with a beauty pageant contestants' night out. Again, I found it very hard to find an available limousine, even though I started my search fairly early. In spite of my efforts, by 4:00 p.m. the day of the celebration (which was to begin at 6:00 p.m.!!), I had still not found an available limousine.

I finally negotiated a deal with a limousine company that involved giving them publicity in addition to payment. I got lucky just in time, but these two experiences highlighted that there was a need for limo service on the island.

Another thing that motivated me to go down the "limousine path" was that my Mom sometimes needs assistance with transportation. She calls me for help, I think because my schedule is flexible. Normally, I put her and all other family needs as first priority.

This was put to the test one day, when I was being sworn in as the President of the new Million Dollar Chapter of BNI. She called me just minutes before this ceremony began, with a request to pick her up and take Dad to the hospital. He was having a reaction to some medication. I suggested that Mom call an ambulance, but she was uncomfortable with this idea. I called my sister Lerry and, fortunately she was able to help out.

Following this, I thought, how nice it would be if I had a limousine and driver available who I could call to help out in such circumstances. That, plus the opportunity for a money-making enterprise that filled a need in the community, led me to pursue, with my husband's blessing, this new business.

Once again, I was discouraged from pursuing this venture! I thought there was a need, so I shared my idea with my friends and they said, "Oh, it will be too expensive and will cost a fortune to maintain. Why don't you just partner with another limo company? The overhead and employee expenses will be too much!"

But, I decided that what I could conceive in my mind, and believe in my heart, I could achieve. I knew I had to give it a try. If it worked, then great! If it did not, then at least I tried. Why are people so afraid to try?!

We call the limousine service *Joni's Paradise Limousine Service*. Most of our clients have been celebrities, as it should be. We have driven Mrs. Hawaii, Mrs. America, the President and Founder of the Mrs. World pageant and the Victor Awards, Olympic Gold Medalists, and a winner of Dancing with the Stars.

If I had listened to doubts, there is no way I would have met all these people. I continue to meet special individuals and make new friends through the limousine service. It has expanded my network tremendously, which in turn helps all my business interests.

Write a book? Who me?

At the end of May 2006, I went to visit Charles Degala, a good friend of mine who is also on the Board of Directors for FAMES. I asked him if he was going to attend the next FAMES meeting and if he would bring a special guest. He looked through his business cards, found one, and said excitedly, "Joni, you need to call Dr. Richard Schuttler! He can be one of our motivational speakers!"

I called him the following day to arrange a luncheon. I scheduled him as a speaker, but unfortunately we were not able to have lunch until after he came to speak for FAMES. That was also the night I had him join the Million Dollar Chapter of BNI. After BNI, I again asked him to lunch. I guess I felt bad because he had written three checks in one night: two for FAMES and one for BNI. I thought I better take him to lunch after all that!

We ate at Dave & Busters and had a great conversation. I shared my background with him and how I had come from humble beginnings. He had watched how I conducted the FAMES and BNI meetings, and asked me how I did it all.

I excitedly responded, "It's my million dollar attitude!"

He quickly said, "Have you thought of writing a book?"

I said I never really thought about it and that I did not know how to get started on something like that.

He said, "I can help you, if you like."

I was surprised to hear that from him and asked, "Do you think that I have a good story to tell?"

He said, "Absolutely!"

I said, "Let's do it!"

He told me to start writing down whatever came into my mind. He also suggested I get a tape recorder and my husband surprised me with a digital recorder. It came in handy! Truthfully, I could not have done this without Tom. He is a considerate and supportive husband. I think because he lived in Mindanao in the provinces of the Philippines, he could better understand what I went through.

Later we had lunch again with Dr. Schuttler and a gentleman who we were considering as a contributing editor. This man asked Dr. Schuttler why he thought my story would be a good book.

He replied, "It seems like everything Joni does turns into gold."

When I heard that, I thought, "Wow! Does he really think that about me?" That was a really nice thing for him to say.

I am blessed that my friend Charles Degala insisted that I call Dr. Schuttler. If Charles had not given me Richard's business card, there wouldn't have been a book!

Be open to new opportunities

You never know what life has in store for you. What if I had not been on that elevator? What if my Mom did not call me for a ride? What if Charles did not share Dr. Schuttler's card with me? What if…?

It's true: things happen for a reason.

The point is you must be open to new opportunities. They are all around you. That is why people say I am creative, adventurous, and willing to take risks.

I say, "Have a can-do attitude, or better yet, a *Million Dollar Attitude!*"

CHAPTER 12
How Do You Do It All?

Joni believes, "It is better to be
rich and tired, rather than poor and bored!"

"You will be made rich in every way so that
you can be generous on every occasion,
and through us your generosity will
result in thanksgiving to God."

2 Corinthians 9:11

Spiritually, Mentally, and Physically Fit

Friends often confess to me their desire to quit their day jobs.
They describe how stressed and unhappy they are and that they
want more out of their lives. Some do not have enough money to
do extra activities or go on vacations with their family. They ask
me what business they might go into to improve their lives.

I normally respond with a few questions:

What do you like to do?

What do you enjoy doing?

What are you passionate about?

I suggest that the answers to these three questions will lead them in the right direction. The money will eventually come if they work hard.

Follow your passion – I tell them!

When they ask me how I do all that I have done and do daily, I respond, "If you enjoy what you are doing, you will never work a day in your life." But, more than that, I believe that in order to be productive and function properly, one must have to be spiritually, mentally, and physically fit.

Mary Kay says to put God first. When people do not do that, they are not balanced. An unshakeable faith is important to overcome doubts, fears, and worries. I never worry! Worrying wastes more energy than working towards a solution. Each morning when I wake up, I thank God for my blessings and I pray for my children, my husband, my parents, my sisters and their families, my friends, and whoever needs His help the most. And, I ask God to continue to give me strength, energy, health, and courage. I also do the same thing at night before I go to sleep.

Being mentally fit means being happy and having the right attitude. I say, "Be happy, it doesn't cost you a penny. When you're not happy, it can cost you plenty!"

I honestly do not understand why people are not happy--- or, rather, why they STAY unhappy instead of working to solve their problems. Perhaps they are not happy because of a bad relationship.

But, why?

Did they not choose that partner? And, if they chose unwisely or if things did not turn out the way they planned, why do they not change the situation?

Maybe they are not happy at work.

But, why?

Are they not free to find other, more meaningful, employment? Maybe they are unhappy because they do not have enough money.

But, why?

Do they not see how the choices they have made led to their current circumstances, and can they not work their way to prosperity by making better choices?

I am not suggesting it is easy. If you think it has been easy for me, go back and read this book again! But, I am saying that there are always solutions to every problem. Setbacks are temporary as long as one keeps working towards one's goals. What's important, of course, is attitude. And, attitude is free!

Allan Silva, a Resource Teacher with the Hawaii State Department of Education is the founder of Positive Connections. He once showed me how attitude is 100% of one's success. He wrote out the word "ATTITUDE" and pointed out that the letter "A" is the first letter of the alphabet, so he gave it a value of 1. The letter "T" is the twentieth letter, so it has a value of 20. The letter "I" is 9, the letter "U" is 21, the letter "D" is 4, and the letter "E" is 5. Then, he told me to add it up. It looked something like this:

A = 1
T = 20
T = 20
I = 9
T = 20
U = 21
D = 4
E = 5
----

100 % of your success is ATTITUDE!

Alter your attitude and you can alter the course of your life.

It is also important to take care of yourself physically. I urge my friends to develop wellness habits such as eating sensibly (although I do love my rice!), getting regular exercise, and taking high-quality vitamin and mineral supplements. I keep chewable Vitamin C tablets with me, and if I feel as if I might be catching a cold, I chew about six or eight of them. The next day, I am as good as new.

Every morning, I exercise. I do my bending and stretching exercises, as well as deep breathing. I do 50 sit-ups in the morning and 50 at night. I do isometrics, a little aerobics, and yoga. After that, I'm ready to go! I also enjoy working out at *Curves* (owned by my friend and BNI chapter member, Gina Richardson) because it is a location for only women and they provide individual specialized attention. The workout energizes me even more.

I also listen to uplifting music whenever I can, especially in the car. A good song can change my mood faster than I can do it on my own.

As a woman, I believe I must make and take time to feed myself spiritually, mentally, and physically. And, for best results, use only positive ingredients!

Get the Children Involved

Another question I am often asked is how I manage to take care of my children and family responsibilities in addition to my career and community service activities. I admit it is not always easy. I used to feel guilty when I had to go to a facial/glamour make-over appointment and my daughter, Jessica, then two years old, cried her heart out, screaming for me. I felt so bad, but I told myself my work was for the family's benefit.

At a Mary Kay seminar, an executive director shared how she felt guilty also leaving her children to go to work. Then she was taught (by a top Mary Kay National Sales Director) to show catalogs and magazines to her children and ask them what toy they would like or where they would like to go for vacation. She said to tell the children that "Mommy is going to work and make money so we can save up for the things you want."

I asked Jessica if she would like to go to Disneyland and she said, "Yes!"

I said, "That's great. When Mommy goes to work, please do not cry anymore because I will be working to save money for our trip to Disneyland."

That really did the trick! She was so happy. After that, when I would leave to go to work she would give me a big hug and kiss and say, "Bye, Mommy. Drive carefully."

I'm happy to say we went to Disneyland twice and once to Walt Disney World.

Jessica and my son, Jason, used to help me with the Mary Kay boxes. Jason would bring them into the house and Jessica would help me sort the contents. She would classify them by colors and shapes. I would ask her to count the tall boxes or the short boxes. I felt that we were spending quality time together and educating the children at the same time.

As Jessica grew older, I would bring her to my Mary Kay appointments – I included her in my work. She quickly learned the steps for good skin care. She would play with the make-up trays while I was finishing with the clients. In the car, while going to appointments, we would 'talk story' and laugh. I cherished those moments.

Little Pitchers have Big Ears

One of the advantages of having a home-based Mary Kay business was that I did not always have to be away from my children while I worked. I made many telephone calls to clients and beauty consultants from my home. I gave a lot of encouragement and pep talks to my sales team. I did not realize that Jason and Jessica were picking up on my positive language and attitude, until one day Jason spilled liquid soap in the bathroom near my work desk while I was speaking to someone on the telephone. I asked him to clean it up, but he said that he did not know how.

I said, "Yes, you can."

He said, "No, I can't."

I said, "Yes, you can."

He said, "No…"

We went back and forth like this a few times, and then all of a sudden he was quiet. A few minutes later, he came out from the bathroom and said, "Mommy, you are right. If you think you can do it, you can! I already cleaned the floor."

"Of course," I replied. "I knew you could do it!"

On another occasion, when Jessica was only four, she and I were alone in the house having lunch. At that time we had a big parrot that somehow managed to get out of its cage. I was always afraid of this bird and when I saw it loose, I started screaming. Jessica screamed, too, and climbed on top of the dining table. I did not know what to do.

I thought, "How can I put this big bird back inside its cage?"

I was terrified, but thinking quickly, I grabbed the broomstick and started to follow the parrot around the family room. Jessica and I both screamed with each stroke as I tried to "sweep" the bird back into its cage.

Jessica kept saying, "You can do it, Mommy! You can do it!"

Finally, I was able to get the parrot in the cage and close the door. My heart was pounding and I was out of breath.

Jessica said, "See, Mommy, you did it! I am so proud of you."

Then, as we hugged each other, I realized she had heard me say this many times to my beauty consultants "You can do it!" When my beauty consultants set personal and sales goals, I told them:

You can do it!

Yes, you can!

When they reached their goals, I'd say,

I'm so proud of you!

In both situations, Jessica and Jason were not just echoing back my words to me; they were beginning to develop their own *Million Dollar Attitude*. I wonder if we as parents fully realize what our children learn from us.

A Winner's Blueprint

I love it when a friend or colleague says to me, "Joni, I want what you have. You're so lucky! I want to be like you."

I say, "Great! Let's get to work."

And, that is when I lose them.

I try to explain what they need to do to achieve their goals, and how they need to plan and schedule appointments with the right people. I tell them it is not that I am that smart, but these things are common sense. However, it seemed that when I would propose a course of action, the excuses would begin:

"That's too far."

"My husband does not want me to go out at night."

"I can not make it that night; I have to watch my shows."

"My appointment cancelled! I am so frustrated!"

"The client did not buy anything. I am going to quit!"

And on and on and on.

I felt sorry for them and I wondered how they are going to reach their goals without taking any action. I offer as much encouragement as I can, and I pray for them. But, I can not make it happen *FOR* them. They have to want it for themselves and then do it for themselves.

I share with them one of my favorite inspirational poems by the late Dr. William Arthur Ward:

A WINNER'S BLUEPRINT FOR ACHIEVEMENT

Believe while others are doubting.
Plan while others are playing.
Study while others are sleeping.
Decide while others are delaying.

Prepare while others are daydreaming.
Begin while others are procrastinating.
Work while others are wishing.
Listen while others are talking.
Smile while others are pouting.

Commend while others are criticizing.
Persist while others are quitting.

This was passed on to me by my Mary Kay Sales Director, Perlita Ancheta, and I have always cherished the words. I wish I had known Dr. Ward while he was alive; I want to thank him for inspiring me. I would have asked him to add one more line to the poem:

Make a million dollars while
others are making a million excuses!

Now, Follow YOUR Dreams

I hope you have found something of value in my story. If so, I invite you to contact me and share your progress. I want to hear YOUR success story. Your determination, persistence, and commitment will take you on an incredible journey.

To summarize my philosophy of life:

Keep thinking,
Keep trying,
Keep failing,
Keep succeeding,
Keep growing,
Keep sharing.

I sincerely encourage you, with all my heart, to press forward and strive to improve yourself on a daily basis and work to build your inner strength. Follow your dreams – do not let anyone stop you.

The Challenge:

THE CHALLENGE

Blessed is the one, indeed,
Who in this life can find
A purpose to fill days,
And goals to fill the mind!

The world is filled with little men,
Content with where they are
Not knowing joys success can bring,
No will to go that far!

Yet, in this world there is a need
For some to lead the rest
To rise above the "average" life,
By giving of their best!

Would you be one, who dares to try,
When challenged by the task
To rise to heights you've never seen,
Or is that too much to ask?

This is your day---a world to win,
Great purpose to achieve
Accept the challenge of your goals
And in yourself, believe!

You will be proud of what you've done,
When at the close of day
You look back on your battle won,
Content, you came this way!

(Author unknown)

I challenge you to acquire, develop, and then demonstrate a *MILLION DOLLAR ATTITUDE.*
I know you can do it.
I believe in you!

God bless you.
Much aloha,
Joni B. Redick-Yundt

ABOUT THE AUTHOR
Joni B. Redick-Yundt

Joni B. Redick-Yundt lives in Honolulu, Hawaii with her husband, Tom Yundt, and her two children, Jason and Jessica. She balances her family with her work at Guardian Life Insurance Company of America, with her work as a Team Leader with Mary Kay Cosmetics, and with her duties as the owner of Joni's Paradise Limousine Services. Joni was chosen as one of the Top 5 Most Intriguing Individuals by *IN Magazine Hawaii* in 2006.

Joni is the President and Founder of FAMES, a nonprofit organization that offers valuable services to the Honolulu business community. Joni is a past-President and the founder of the Million Dollar Chapter of BNI Hawaii.

Joni's extensive community service includes:

★ 2001-Present: *Hawaii Skin Cancer Coalition/American Cancer Society* committee member.
★ 2004: *Hawaii Skin Cancer Coalition* President. Assisted doctors, organization and local schools to educate the public regarding sun protection awareness, and provide free skin cancer screening to the public.
★ 2001-Present: *Mother Earth Environmental Charity Foundation*. Served as Vice President in 2003-2004 and Director in 2005-present; and, as 2001 Chairperson for the Toys-For-Tots program. Adopted highway for cleanup efforts.

★ 1998: *Juvenile Diabetes Foundation*. Recipient of the "Golden Sneaker" award for raising funds to find a cure for juvenile diabetes.

★ 2002-2006: *Sisters Offering Support*. Executive Advisory Board. Provided assistance and raised funds to help sexually exploited young women.

★ 2001: *Child Abuse Prevention* volunteer.

★ 2004: *American Heart Association*. 'Queen of Heart' 1st runner up, raised nearly $10,000 to help the organization fight heart disease and strokes in Hawaii.

★ 2002-Present: *Hawaii State Sheriff Association*. Helped to promote community understanding for law enforcement in the State of Hawaii and share in the Aloha Spirit by providing financial support.

★ 2004-Present: *Hawaii's Most Wanted Law Enforcement Organization*. President, 2004; Vice-President, 2005-present. Publishes a magazine that contains information about almost all law enforcement, crime prevention, safety tips, community resources and business advertisers.

★ 1996-2005: Volunteer, Mililani Elementary School and Mililani Intermediate School.

★ 2004: *Kamehameha Schools*. Chairperson for corporate sponsors, scholarship golf tournament.

★ 2004-Present: *Honolulu Broadway Babies*. Promotions and Marketing; to provide fundraising for children with disabilities.

★ 2004-2005: *Miss Oahu Filipina Pageant*. Corporate sponsor, provided a car to the winner to use for one year.

★ 2003-2005: *Miss Hawaii Filipina*. Chairperson for corporate sponsorships.

★ 2007: *Mrs. Hawaii United States Pageant*. Volunteer in providing services: printing, limousines, emcee, judges, and venue.

★ 2001: *St. John's Apostle and Evangelist Church*. Volunteer and assistant auditor.

Joni is a motivational speaker at, and supporter of, various business, school, and community events. Joni can be contacted via email at jonimda@yahoo.com.

Dr. Richard Schuttler

Dr. Richard Schuttler is an international public speaker, consultant, educator, and author. As a consultant, he makes available motivational, team building, and leadership improvement expertise with academic, federal/state governments, and Fortune 1,000 environments. Dr. Schuttler operates *Organizational Troubleshooter, LLC,* from two locations in Phoenix, Arizona and Honolulu, Hawaii. He can be reached via the Internet via http://www.orgtroubleshooter.org.

Contributing Writers And Editors

THOMAS "TOM" C. YUNDT, Senior Aviation Engineer.

SANDY C. McKEE, J.D., is a writer and entrepreneur with various business interests. She is the current President of the Kaimuki Chapter of BNI Hawaii and is the Hawaii Bureau Chief and writer for the online magazine The National Networker (www. thenationalnetworker.com).

What Others Have To Say About Joni

"Joni has a heart of gold, and her endless giving is what makes her one of a kind. This book is highly recommended to give the reader a more valuable and meaningful life."

Cynthia Aiu, Mrs. Hawaii United States 2006
Editor-in-Chief and Founder
Hawaii Mrs. Magazine

"Joni's persistence and belief in herself has allowed her to inspire others to achieve their goals, both personally and professionally. Her *Million Dollar Attitude* is a winner!"

David Akina
Founder, The Paradise Yellow Pages

"Some very close friends insisted that I meet Joni---this young, vibrant, brilliant career woman whom they said is someone that would impress me even more as I get to know her better. She is a living example of her work in her new book *Million Dollar Attitude*. I believe that this book will benefit people of all ages and all walks of life---students or teachers, workers, entrepreneurs, stay-at-home parents, retirees, kids, teens, parents, young adults, or seniors--- everyone can benefit from the wisdom in this book."

Michelle Alarcon, J.D., M.B.A.
Asst. Professor of Management
College of Business Administration
Hawaii Pacific University

"Joni's attributes: ambitious, sets high goals, big thinker, achiever, smart, hardworking, shoots for the moon, charming and beautiful, sees good in others, inspires and encourages others to achieve, radiates excitement, positive mental attitude, and successful. Congratulations, Joni, for caring and sharing your wonderful attributes and God-given abilities with the whole world. Reaching out to people through your book could make a difference in their lives!"

Pearl M. Ancheta
Ind. Mary Kay Sales Director

"Joni Redick-Yundt, the consummate entrepreneur, is an inspiration and shares her secrets to success in her new book."

Rob Bertholf, Founder/CEO
Empowered Internet Solutions
Hawaii and Florida

"Joni's energy and enthusiasm makes her a genuine spark plug in the community. She truly knows how to make things happen."

Richard Chan
Owner, I Love Country Cafe

"I've personally witnessed Joni go through painstaking challenges in her life and she has always turned everything to positive. She is relentless, tireless, and fearless. She has all the ingredients to succeed because of her winning attitude. If we can learn and pick up one or two things from her book and put it to practice, we'll be on the road to success."

Mary L. Cordero
Publisher, Fil-Am Courier

"Aloha, Joni! I just want to thank you for everything. You have been a great friend. I learned so many things from you."

Cherryl Lyn Cunanan
Regional Manager, HelmsBriscoe

"A woman with an effervescent personality and everlasting energy, she truly serves above self with her major contributions to the communities of Hawaii."

Charles Degala
President/Owner Pacific Coast Capital
and Entertainer for Tihati Productions

"Ralph Waldo Emerson, who said, "What lies behind us and what lies before us are tiny matters compared to what lies within us," defines the power of character I see in Joni Redick-Yundt. Joni is a woman of substance who carries through what she is able to do. Her winning attitude, good heart and good will are wonderful reflections on humanity."

Faye Dela Cruz, Early Childhood Educator
Tacoma, Washington

"Joni takes time out to make relationships work in a personal way, and that's one of the things that helps her get so much done. Her professional presentation, smile, and ability to accomplish a variety of projects all at one time are inspirational."

Linda Dela Cruz
Website Editor and Senior Writer
Midweek Magazine
and U.S. Small Business Administration
2007 Small Business Journalist
of the Year for Oahu

"Joni one of the most beautiful women in Hawaii, with boundless energy. She's absolutely amazing. She's involved in just about anything in Hawaii. The biggest thing about Joni is her positive outlook in life. She's one of a few people who has a total CAN-DO attitude. I unequivocally recommend Joni's *Million Dollar Attitude* book especially for corporations and companies that have challenges with their employees."

Ben Dowling
Vice President and Co-Owner,
Nick's Fishmarket

"I have always known Joni as a positive, strong-minded person, and a good role model. She's a great mentor and inspiration to a lot of men and women. More power to you, Joni! Your book is something that I will recommend to all my friends."

Eliza Edralin
Realtor, Las Vegas, Nevada

"Joni is a dynamic and talented woman, and I have confidence in her new endeavor."

Naomi Hazelton-Giambrone
Publisher and Owner, Pacific Edge Magazine
And Ko Olina Life & Style Magazine

"I have always been impressed by Joni's never-ending perseverance and positive attitude. She is living proof that you can achieve your dreams if you believe in yourself."

Erwin Hudelist
President and CEO, Hagadone Printing

"Joni is an incredible example of true leadership, determination, and success for all women. Her determination is nothing short of amazing. She doesn't keep her success to herself. Instead, she is spreading the wealth as she shares her knowledge with those around her."

Angela Keen, News 8 Today Anchor
KHNL News 8, NBC Honolulu

"I have known Joni for over twenty years and have watched her grow into a wonderful community and civic leader. She has an enormous capacity for caring and compassion, and at the same time, shows great skills in business and people management. Joni dedicates 110% to whatever she undertakes. It would be hard to find another person with such talents and fine personal qualities as Joni."

Tai Khan
Owner, Zaffron Indian Restaurant
and Food Quality Analysts

"Joni's story embodies today's new American Dream. Not only for those who have immigrated to our shores, but for all those who strive for more!"

Peter and Nikky Leahey
Boston, Massachusetts

"Is this lady for real...positive, enthusiastic, hardworking, kind-hearted, giving, smart, successful, trustworthy, Godly, genuine, appreciative, selfless, humble, AND beautiful? The answer is YES and much more! With her new book, Joni will inspire, touch, and move individuals like myself to have a better quality of life, gain success, and overcome challenges with a positive *Million Dollar Attitude*. From the first time I met Joni, she's been such a blessing in my life---an answer to my prayer. I am proud to call her *Ate* (big sister in Filipino)."

Kristian Lei
Christian Recording Artist
and Founder of Honolulu Broadway Babies
formerly "Miss Saigon"

"In *Million Dollar Attitude*, Joni gives her readers a variety of strategies and techniques for developing a winning attitude that yields success. Picking up this book implies that you understand how a great attitude can help drive you."

Paul K. Lemcke
Vice President and Loan Officer
Ohana Pacific Bank, Honolulu, Hawaii

"We are proud and honored at Dave and Buster's to have been associated with Joni, FAMES, and BNI for the past two years. Joni is truly an inspiration to everyone she comes into contact with. She is an incredibly talented person who has a true zest for life and it shows with her *Million Dollar Attitude!*

Matt Luckett
General Manager, Dave and Buster's
Honolulu, Hawaii

"We met Joni through FAMES and have been astounded by the amount of growth in this young organization in such a short period of time. FAMES is the brainchild of Joni and she provides the spark of vitality that is behind its success. Her vision, drive, and positive energy make for a powerful combination. Joni does what she says she's going to do, and because of that we will continue to support her."

Rosalinda Rosacia and Eugene C. Malalis
Owners, Nightingale Case Management

"Joni Redick-Yundt has a 'Million Dollar Personality' to go along with her *Million Dollar Attitude* about family, work, and community. She is a winner in my book."

John Noland, Talk Show Host and Producer
K-108 Radio Station

"The story about Joni is simply incredible and delightfully magical. How else can one describe some one who continues to express her natural, gifted, talents with challenging accomplishments that inspire everyone, everywhere!"

Roger Ogata, M.D.
Wellness Concepts

"I highly recommend Joni Redick-Yundt's *Million Dollar Attitude* book. She is a make-a-difference person with a mind that is always churning and striving to uplift others. I was drawn to her Aloha Spirit when I first met her and knew she was a community leader with a passion to help others."

Beulah Olanolan
Asst. Vice President and
Business Banking Officer
Bank of Hawaii

"I have never known anyone who does so many tasks at the same time and stays on top of everything. With Joni's *Million Dollar Attitude*, she does it all."

Walter Peters, President
Mortgage Free Americans

"Joni, keep showing and encouraging women with your *Million Dollar Attitude*, and thank you for being a blessing."

Gina M. Richardson
Owner, Curves in Waipio and Wahiawa, Hawaii

"From the very first time I met Joni, I knew she had tremendous strength and determination, so it did not surprise me that when she set a goal to start a BNI chapter, how impressive it would be. Joni's *Million Dollar Attitude* formed the Million Dollar Chapter. This chapter is the largest chapter ever started in Hawaii. The chapter kicked off with 50 members and in the first five weeks generated over $800,000 in business for its members. Now, that is Joni at work!"

Joann Seery
Executive Director, BNI Hawaii

"A *Million Dollar Attitude* will give you golden opportunities you never dreamed of! It is great to read a book by someone who actually walks her talk. Great job, Wonder Woman."

Allan Silva
Founder, Positive Connections
and Resource Teacher
Department of Education, State of Hawaii

"Joni is such an impressive individual. Always on point, never losing focus of the outcome of what she has set out to do. I have known her for a few years now, and she has conquered more goals in the last few years than many get to in a lifetime. Her drive, enthusiasm and energy are contagious. I hope the secrets are in this book! Affecting all that surround her, Joni is nothing less than inspiring."

David Silva
President, Revolution Motorsports

"Joni's million dollar smile and her attitude certainly matches the title of her book. She is herself one in a million. What more can I say!!"

Dr. Lawrence K.W. Tseu, DDS Inc.
Jackie Chan Charitable Foundation, USA-President
Board of Regents – University of Oxford, England

"Joni B. Redick-Yundt exudes confidence, intelligence, and an unwavering passion to help others. Those coveted personal attributes have been captured in this book. It is a must read for anyone with a desire to succeed in business, and in life."

Glenn Wakai
Hawaii State Representative
Moanalua-Salt Lake Aliamanu

"Joni has always inspired me over the years with her million dollar attitude. It is people like her who make me believe anything is possible as long as you put your mind to it. When she told me six months ago that she was going to write this book, I was not surprised nor had I any doubts that she could do it. Congratulations to Joni! To her continued success..."

Peter Philipp Wingsoe, Co-Owner
EFG::Entertainment Fusion Group
West Hollywood, California

Printed in the United States
117470LV00005B/184-768/A

9 781434 318275